D1271059

ENCYCLOPEDIA OF MAMMALS

VOLUME 2
Bat–Bea

MARSHALL CAVENDISH

NEW YORK • LONDON • TORONTO • SYDNEY

J. LEWIS CROZER LIBRARY

FRUIT BATS

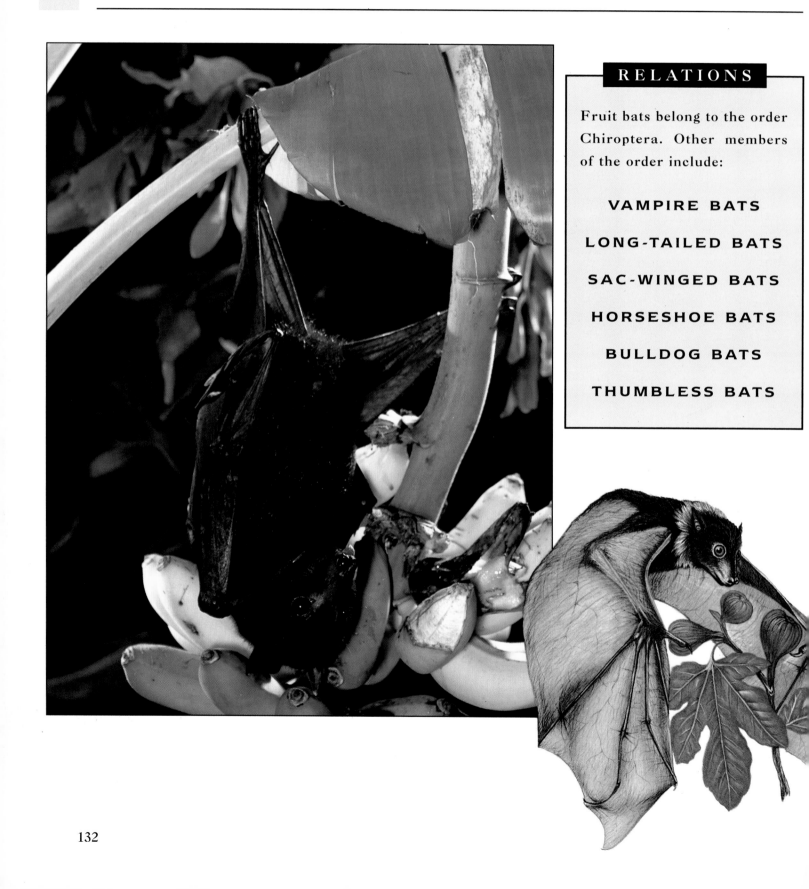

Fruit bats belong to the order Chiroptera. Other members of the order include:

VAMPIRE BATS

LONG-TAILED BATS

SAC-WINGED BATS

HORSESHOE BATS

BULLDOG BATS

THUMBLESS BATS

Merlin D.Tuttle/Oxford Scientific Films

CLASSIFICATION

Fruit bats, like all bats,
belong to the large
mammalian order
Chiroptera. They are
usually large bats with
dense fur. Fruit bats
are split off from the
majority of bats and are
placed in the suborder
Megachiroptera. This
suborder contains just
one large family, the
Pteropodidae. There are
173 species of fruit bat,
split up between 42
living genera.

ORDER
Chiroptera
(bats)

SUBORDER
Megachiroptera
(Old World fruit bats)

FAMILY
Pteropodidae
(fruit bats)

SUBFAMILY
Pteropodinae
(fruit-eating bats)

SUBFAMILY
Macroglossinae
(long-tongued bats)

GIANT FLYING VEGETARIANS

OLD WORLD FRUIT BATS ARE THE LARGEST AND MOST POWERFUL OF ALL THE FLYING MAMMALS. BUT DESPITE THEIR LARGE SIZE, RAZOR-SHARP CLAWS, AND KEEN EYESIGHT, THEY FEED ALMOST WHOLLY ON FRUIT, POLLEN, AND NECTAR

Bats are generally disliked for various reasons, not least of which being that they are often linked with the supernatural and figure highly in horror stories. Strangely, however, despite their typically large size, most fruit bats manage to avoid this reputation, and in some parts of the world they are revered as lucky or even holy. Some even manage to have a positive image. Probably, the most obvious reason for this is that they have familiar doglike faces, with large, appealing eyes. Also, their vegetarian nature and the fact that some fly during the day make them appear less eerie than their night-flying, carnivorous cousins.

THE BAT FAMILY

All bats belong to the large group of mammals called chiropterans (ky-ROP-ta-runs). To date, over 980 species of bat have been identified, and more are discovered every year. This highly successful group has

133

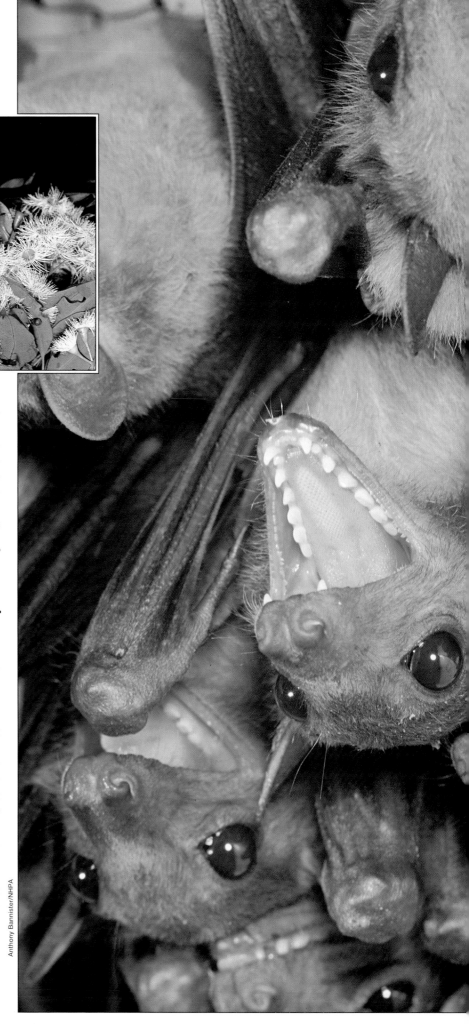

A gray-headed flying fox or fruit bat enjoys a favorite meal of eucalyptus flowers (below).

Ken Griffiths/NHPA

spread throughout the world.

Bats are split into two smaller groups, or sub-orders, Megachiroptera (MEG-a-ky-rop-ta-ruh), or big bats, and the Microchiroptera (MY-cro-ky-rop-ta-ruh), or small bats. However, these names are slightly misleading as not all of the big bats are larger than the small bats. Luckily, size is not the only reason these two groups are separate.

Fruit bats are placed in the "big bat" group, but

BATS ARE THE ONLY MAMMALS WITH WINGS THAT FLAP AND CAN UNDERTAKE POWERED FLIGHT

---

they differ from most other bats in several ways. One of the characteristics most commonly associated with bats is their ability to locate objects using echolocation. Fruit bats have not developed the use of echolocation to anywhere near the same extent as bats that feed on insects.

Because of this, their faces have retained what are generally considered mammalian features. For example, they have not had to develop the complex ears and leaflike nasal projections of the small bats. Instead, they rely on their excellent eyesight and keen sense of smell to locate their food and avoid obstacles.

Another major difference between fruit bats and most other bats is that they are not carnivores, but fruit- and flower-eating herbivores. Most species squeeze the juices out of the soft flesh of ripe fruit, while others have become more

Fruit bats, such as these Egyptian fruit bats, have large, forward-facing eyes and doglike features.

Anthony Bannister/NHPA

134

M.Ellanby/Natural Science Photos

specialized and will feed only on pollen and nectar.

Other differences include a claw between their thumb, which sticks out halfway along the front edge of their wing, and the tip of the wing. This is used to good effect during male territorial disputes.

The fruit bats are themselves split into two subfamilies. The largest of these two groups contains 158 species. It is made up of the fruit-eating bats and is called Pteropodinae (te-ro-PO-din-ay). The second group, which is called Macroglossinae (MAC-ro-GLOSS-in-ay), contains only 15 species of bat. The bats in this group have tongues that are generally longer than those of the fruit-eating bats. These long-tongued bats are usually much smaller than their fruit-eating relatives.

MYSTERIOUS PAST

Very little is known about how the modern bat evolved and even less is known about the evolution of the fruit bats. It is speculated that bats are of monophyletic origin, meaning that bats radiated from a single common ancestor. However, there is no direct evidence for this. Trying to work out the evolution of the fruit bats is even more complex as they appear to share many characteristics with the primates. Studies of their brains, as well as other characteristics, suggest that they might have evolved independently of the small bats. Evidence indicates that they may actually have split from the early ancestors of the primates. However, recent studies of the material that carries the genetic information

A fruit bat hanging from a creeper in a West African rain forest.

that is unique to all species, DNA, suggests a closer link with the bats' group.

What is known, however, is that during the 10 million years after the last of the dinosaurs became extinct, many ecological niches became available. This was an amazing period of time when most mammal groups appeared, from bats to baleen whales. However, as absolutely no fossil evidence of fruit bats has been discovered from this time, it is impossible to tell whether the two orders of bat evolved independently or from a common ancestor.

Like most mammal groups that rushed to fill the ecological gaps left by the great extinction at the end of the Cretaceous period, bats evolved surprisingly quickly. Yet how they developed wings is still unclear.

Bats may have begun their evolution looking

THE OLDEST REMAINS OF IDENTIFIABLE FRUIT BATS WERE FOUND IN SEVERAL PLACES IN EUROPE AND ARE ABOUT THREE MILLION YEARS OLD

---

similar to modern-day flying squirrels and, over several million years, evolved the membranous wings they have today. They thrived on a plentiful diet of winged insects, which had few other predators, especially at night.

However, why fruit-eating mammals should need to fly as well as fruit bats do is less clear. Possibly the need to find fruit that had just ripened forced these mammals to travel large distances, and gliding from tree to tree was probably the quickest and least dangerous way.

At the beginning of the fruit bats' evolution the climate of the world was much warmer and they could be found much farther north than they can at present. Today, because most fruit bats need a constant supply of freshly ripened fruit, they can only survive in the tropics. ∎

NOSING AHEAD

Although strange-shaped noses are typical of the small insect-feeding bats, they are rare in the fruit bats. The Southeast Asian tube-nosed fruit bat has a pair of 0.3-in-(7-mm)-long fleshy growths that extend beyond the face. At present their specific use is unknown, but when other bats start to call, or if there is a sudden disturbance nearby, these projections begin to quiver and move from side to side. In this way they appear to act like radar dishes and might be used in ultrasonic communication.

THE FRUIT BATS' FAMILY TREE

Because bats are one of the least understood groups of mammals, it is very difficult to work out exactly which groups are more closely related than others. Also, as nearly one-quarter of all mammals are bats, there are a large number of surprisingly varied species to list. To confuse things even more, several species are known from only one individual, and new species are always being discovered. However, fruit bats are only found in the Old World, which stretches from Europe through Asia, Africa, and Australia.

GRAY-HEADED FLYING FOX
Pteropus poliopcephalus
(te-RO-pus PO-lee-o-SE-FA-lus)

The gray-headed fruit bat, also known as the gray-headed or Australian big-headed flying fox, belongs to the genus Pteropus, which is made up of 59 different species and contains some of the largest of all bats. The gray-headed fruit bat has the large eyes and long, doglike features typical of these large bats. It has an extra pair of claws and no tail. They have varied fur color ranging from gray through brown to black.

All Illustrations Rachel Lockwood/Wildlife Art Agency

ALL BATS
Chiroptera
(ky-ROP-ta-ruh)

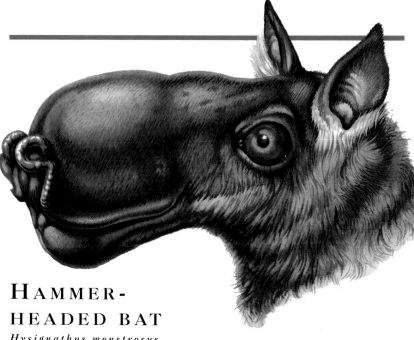

HAMMER-HEADED BAT

Hysignathus monstrosus

(hi-sig-NAY-thus mon-STRO-sus)

There is only one species of bat in the genus Hysignathus and that is the hammer-headed fruit bat (Hysignathus monstrosus). The male cannot be mistaken for any other bat, as its whole body and face have evolved around its massive voice box. The female, however, looks more like a typical fruit bat.

OTHER SPECIES:

EPAULETTED BAT
EPAULETTED FRUIT BAT
DWARF EPAULET-TED BAT
LITTLE FLYING COW
LONG-PALATED FRUIT BAT
SHORT-PALATED FRUIT BAT
DOG-FACED FRUIT BAT
BIG-HEADED DOG-FACED FRUIT BAT

SHORT-TOOTHED DOG-FACED FRUIT BAT
DYAK FRUIT BAT
BLACK-CAPPED FRUIT BAT
DUSKY FRUIT BAT
FISCHER'S PYGMY FRUIT BAT
LONG-HAIRED FRUIT BAT
HAIRY MOUNTAIN FRUIT BAT
HIGH WAVY MOUNTAIN FRUIT BAT

TUBE-NOSED FRUIT BAT

Nyctimene major

(nic-TIE-men-ay MAY-ger)

With 14 species, the genus Nyctimene is one of the largest in the fruit bat subfamily. The tube-nosed fruit bat, Nyctimene major, has the two long nostrils that are typical of this genus. It is possible that some of the bats in this subfamily might be partially insectivorous.

EGYPTIAN BAT

Rousettus aegyptiacus

(roo-SET-us eye-GIP-tee-a-cus)

There are 10 species in the genus Rousettus. The rousette or Egyptian fruit bat is one of the very few species of fruit bat that uses echolocation.

FOX OR FRUIT

Traditionally, it is only those bats that belong to the genus *Pteropus* that are called flying foxes. The term fruit bat is often used to describe all those bats that belong to the family *Pteropodinae* so that they are not confused with the long-tongued bats.

ANATOMY:
THE GRAY-HEADED FRUIT BAT

WING MEMBRANE

The large surface area of the wing membrane is highly elastic and very thin. It is made up of two thin layers of skin. Blood vessels and nerves are sandwiched between these two layers.

FEET

The long claws provide such a secure grip that the fruit bat can hang upside down by one leg and use the other to groom itself. They are also used to grip on to fruit when they feed.

The gray-headed fruit bat or flying fox displays most of the characteristics associated with the fruit bat family. It is one of the largest, with a wingspan of 4 ft (1.2 m). The largest fruit bat is the common fruit bat which has a wingspan of 5.5 ft (1.7 m) and weighs 3.3 lb (1,500 g). The smallest fruit bat, which belongs to the African long-tongued bat genus, has a wingspan of just 10 in (25 cm) and weighs little more than 0.5 oz (14 g).

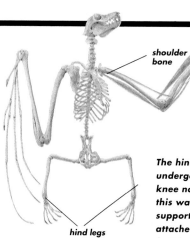

Anatomy illustrations Philip Hood/Wildlife Art Agency

FIVE DIGITS

The fruit bat's finger digits have evolved into long finger bones that support the large membranous wings in the same way as the spokes of an umbrella. Like all bats, fruit bats have a thumb claw; however, they also have a claw on their second finger. The thumb and extra finger claw help support the wing membrane in front of the forearm, which can be quite large in some fruit bats. In some species the males also use this claw to fight with.

THICK FUR

With a high metabolic rate and a vegetarian diet, fruit bats need a thick insulating layer of fur to keep their body heat in. For those fruit bats that live at high altitudes in mountains, this is especially important.

FRUIT BAT SKELETON

To keep the bat's body rigid in flight, several of its neck vertebrae have become fused together. Their ribs have also become flattened, giving the body a more stable and streamlined shape.

shoulder bone

finger bones

The hind limbs have undergone a rotation through 180°. The knee now bends outward and backward. In this way the wing membrane is given extra support during flight. Powerful tendons attached to the bones of the feet give the fruit bat a tight grip.

hind legs

The shoulder bones are considerably more developed than the pelvis. A large and solid collarbone, or clavicle, is fused to the shoulders, adding strength to the upper torso. The breast-bone, or sternum, has a ridge running down its length that allows the powerful flight muscles to be attached firmly.

X-ray Illustrations Elisabeth Smith

GRAY-HEADED FRUIT BAT

CLASSIFICATION

GENUS: *PTEROPUS*

SPECIES: *POLIOCEPHALUS*

SIZE

HEAD–BODY LENGTH/MALE: 11.7 IN (30 CM)

HEAD–BODY LENGTH/FEMALE: 7.8 IN (20 CM)

WEIGHT/MALE: 2.6 LB (1.2 KG)

WEIGHT/FEMALE: 1.8 LB (0.8 KG)

WING SPAN/MALE: 4 FT (1.2 M)

WING SPAN/FEMALE: 2.6 FT (0.8 M)

COLORATION

GROUND COLOR VARIES FROM GRAYISH BROWN TO ALMOST BLACK

A PATCH OF FUR ON THE BACK BETWEEN THE WINGS IS GRAYISH YELLOW

EARS, WINGS, AND NOSE ARE BLACK

EYES ARE REDDISH BROWN

FEATURES

THICK FUR COVERS BODY AND HEAD

PROMINENT, HAIRLESS EARS

LARGE EYES

ELONGATED MUZZLE

FREE–TAILED BAT

MOUSE–TAILED BAT

MOUSE–EARED BAT

SHEATH–TAILED BAT

TUBE–NOSED FRUIT BAT

FLYING FOX

LARGE EYES

Fruit bats have excellent night vision. At the back of all mammalian eyes are special cells called rods. These are used for nighttime vision. Although they are not sensitive to colors, they are highly sensitive to light. In the fruit bat's eyes these rods have fingerlike projections that increase the surface area, enabling the bat's eyes to capture more of the available light. This gives the bat its sharp black-and-white vision in low light levels.

TELLTALE TAILS *(LEFT)*

Bats display a wide variety of tail shapes, and fruit bats are no exception. Usually they are short or nonexistent. Bats that belong to the flying fox genus Pteropus never have a tail. The rousette fruit bat, however, has a short stump of a tail that is rarely longer than 0.8 in (2 cm), while insectivorous bats, such as the mouse-tailed bats of the genus Rhinopoma, have long tails—up to 3.1 in (8 cm)—which hang freely. The lack of tails in fruit bats is another guide to their lifestyle. Because they do not need to chase after swiftly moving prey, they no longer need the rudderlike tail that gives other bats balance in flight.

FRUIT BAT SKULL

Fruit bats have varied skull shapes. Those that feed on flowers tend to have longer and thinner noses. Fruit bats also have many different patterns of teeth. The incisors are small as they have little use for them. Canine teeth are present even in those bats that have taken to a diet of pollen and fruit. The molar teeth are low and widely spaced. The crowns are long, flat, and grooved to help squash the ripe fruit and aid in the removal of seeds and the tough skin of some fruits.

FRUIT BAT CLAW

This cartilaginous spur keeps the tail membrane rigid in flight. In fruit bats it is also used to hold food.

FRUIT FEEDERS

FRUIT BATS ARE THE GIANTS OF THE BAT WORLD. THEY ARE ALSO HIGHLY SOCIABLE AND GATHER IN HUGE NUMBERS. EVERY DUSK THEY TAKE FLIGHT AND PREPARE FOR A NIGHT'S FEASTING ON FRUIT

One of the most amazing sights in the tropics is that of huge roosts of fruit bats as the sun sets and dusk begins. The trees come alive as countless thousands of giant bats take to the air in their nightly search for ripe fruit. However, not all fruit bats behave this way. With over 173 species, they display a wide variety of behaviors, although they share one common characteristic—they are all vegetarians.

Ripe fruit and trees in flower govern the lives of fruit bats. Because of their specialized diet and habit of living in large colonies, they must always remain within flying range of such trees. If an area is stripped of soft fruit, the bats must move on. For this reason most species do not have permanent territories and will migrate from one area to another, often returning to specific trees every year or so.

However, this is not as restricting as it may seem,

FRUIT BATS ARE HIGHLY SKILLED AT "HIT AND RUN" FORAGING—SELECTING FRUIT AND TAKING IT ELSEWHERE TO EAT

as most fruit bats are strong fliers. A night's flying may vary from just a few miles to over 18.6 miles (30 km). Some of the larger species have been known to fly up to 62 miles (100 km) and one particular bat ended its flight on the deck of a ship almost 199 miles (320 km) out to sea!

Fruit bats hang upside down when at rest in the trees. However, they differ from the small bats in that they hold their head at right angles to their body. In line with most bats they are communal animals, so most species form large groups. Some of the larger species, such as the common flying fox, gather in groups of over 250,000 individuals. Sadly, such huge roosts are becoming increasingly rare.

These temporary roosts, or camps as they are

Hans and Judy Beste/Ardea

A black flying fox hanging from a banana tree (above). *Its penchant for cultivated fruit crops has cost Australian fruit growers a lot of time and money.*

also known, might seem disorganized, but within them there is a basic hierarchy. Large, fully grown males are at the top of the pecking order, and the young, independent bats are at the bottom. The main advantage of being high up in the hierarchy is that the bat has pick of the best roosting sites. This is especially important during the mating season.

During the day these roosts are very active and it is at this time that most of the squabbles for the best branches take place. It is a noisy business with much flapping of wings, baring of fangs, and piercing

Anthony Healy/Bruce Coleman Ltd.

Red fruit bats at Windjana Gorge National Park, Kimberley, Australia. During the early evening these bats fill the sky in huge groups of up to 250,000 individuals in their search for food.

screeches. If a roost has been stripped frequently of its leaves, it will eventually die.

Smell is an important sense for fruit bats. Not only does it help them find food, but it also plays an important role within the roost. Male bats produce a strong-smelling scent or musk. This smell probably helps keep the colony together. Sometimes the smell of a large colony can be detected by humans several hundred yards away.

Not all species of fruit bat display this sort of general behavior. Several species make their homes in caves, hollow tree trunks, or under roofs, while one group of fruit bats even prefers to roost in rolled-up banana leaves, and another is often found in old tombs. ■

A lesser tube-nosed fruit bat in New Guinea. The function of its odd-shaped nose is unclear, but its sense of smell is keen.

Roy D. Mackay/NHPA

HABITATS

Fruit bats are only found in the tropics of the Old World, from sub-Saharan Africa, through the Middle East, to the islands of the South Pacific, although the pollen- and nectar-eating species of bat are less widespread. However, within this area they are found in most habitats, including humid swamps, tropical islands, mountain slopes, and even in the homes of people. One of the reasons

---

AUSTRALIAN BIG-HEADED FLYING FOXES CAN MIGRATE UP TO 620 MILES (1,000 KM) IN SEARCH OF FOOD

---

for this is that fruit-bearing trees are common in tropical areas and rely on bats—along with other fruit-eating animals—to spread their seeds. And the lack of seasons in such areas means that there is a year-round food supply for the bats.

Another more obvious reason for their widespread distribution in the tropics is their ability to fly. Apart from birds, they are the only other vertebrates capable of sustained "true" flight. The earliest remains of fruit bats were, in fact, found in the southern parts of Europe. They then spread to Africa, Madagascar, the East Indies, and on through to the South Pacific. Their ability to fly

Straw-colored fruit bats, roosting in a treetop in Sierra Leone (right). *Only large fruit bats do this, using their wings as protection from the elements.*

(in)SIGHT

FRUIT BATS AND WATER

Fruit bats are often found near water. This is because large amounts of water are lost through evaporation from their wings and they must make up for that loss by having a readily available supply. Luckily bats are excellent swimmers, should they fall in, and are able to use their wings to push themselves along the surface.

Another benefit of being able to swim is that it allows the bats to grab fruit that falls into the water. However, they must always be on the lookout for crocodiles, which will not turn up their noses at such a tasty—and opportune—snack!

DISTRIBUTION

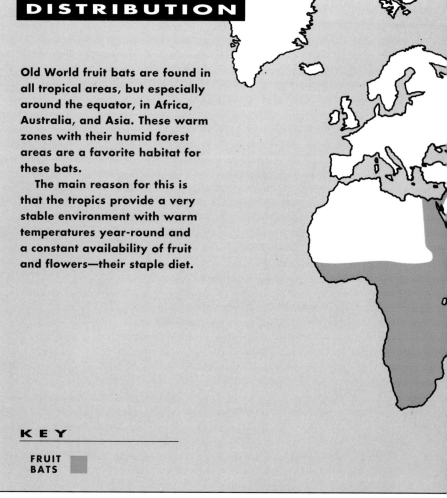

Old World fruit bats are found in all tropical areas, but especially around the equator, in Africa, Australia, and Asia. These warm zones with their humid forest areas are a favorite habitat for these bats.

The main reason for this is that the tropics provide a very stable environment with warm temperatures year-round and a constant availability of fruit and flowers—their staple diet.

KEY

FRUIT BATS ▢

Nick Gordon/Ardea

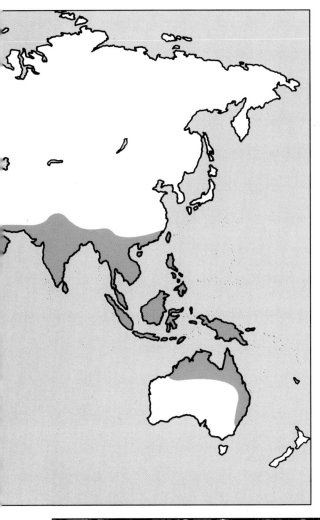

● Some 70 percent of all the living species of fruit bat (over 200 species) are found in the tropical and subtropical areas of Southeast Asia and Indo-Australia alone.

● Old World fruit bats roost in trees and simply navigate by sight. The one exception is the rousette bat which roosts in caves and uses echolocation to move about.

● The larger flying foxes roost in exposed camps in trees, often stripping the leaves for improved visibility. They have no real natural enemies and use their wings against the elements.

Epauletted fruit bats in Africa hanging from wild gardenia (below). *These shy creatures are only found singly or in small numbers.*

long distances, coupled with the strong winds associated with the tropics, led to many bats being blown out to sea. Most would have perished, but occasionally some would have survived to colonize a new area.

But there are restricting factors to the range of the fruit bats, and one of these is their need for fresh water. Bats lose a lot of water through their wing membranes, especially in flight, so they must always have access to plenty of fresh water. They drink by flying down and dipping their mouths in water. But because larger fruit bats are less maneuverable in flight than smaller species, they need a reasonably large stretch of water to do this. Fortunately this is in abundance in tropical areas. ■

Peter Johnson/NHPA

FOOD AND FEEDING

Although fruit bats may occasionally eat insects that are in or on flowers and fruit, no species actively looks for them. And because they have never needed the ability to detect fast-moving prey, only a few species are able to use echolocation—a development that prevents them bumping into bats and other objects. Instead, fruit bats have evolved an excellent sense of smell. When a tree comes into flower or fruit, they can smell it several miles away. Once they have located the approximate area, their sharp nighttime vision allows them to home in on it.

BATS DO NOT DIGEST CELLULOSE IN LEAVES, AS THE PROCESS TAKES TIME AND ADDS WEIGHT TO THEIR BODIES

They also have good eyesight to help them land safely in the dark.

At dusk fruit bats take to the air and start swirling around above their roost. After a few minutes they all head off in the same direction. Fruit bats will travel more than 18 miles (30 km) to a feeding site.

Once a site is located, the fruit bats fly down and start to feed. This is a very noisy and messy business. Squabbles instantly break out over prime feeding perches. Once a piece of fruit has been secured, they hold it between their feet and start to feed. However, most fruit bats do not eat the whole fruit. Instead they suck out the flesh and squeeze it against the ridged bony palate on the roof of their

In flight the bat raises its wings above its body, then brings them down and flicks them forward before raising them again, in a circular movement.

All Illustrations John Cox/Wildlife Art Agency

mouths. They then swallow the juices. So as to extract as much as possible, they also chew each mouthful a few times passing it from cheek to cheek. Eventually, when there is no more juice left, they spit out the remaining skin and pulp. Many species of fruit bat also feed on flowers and use their long tongues to collect all the pollen and nectar.

Fruit bats are also excellent seed dispersers. As they eat, small seeds drip down onto their fur or are swallowed. These will then be carried away from that particular tree to other parts of the forest, and either cleaned from its fur when the bat returns to its roost, or excreted in its own little supply of fertilizer.

In this way bats also fulfill a vital role as pollinators and propagators of the tropical forest. By passing pollen that gets stuck in their fur from one tree to the next, not only do they help the tree reproduce, but they also guarantee that in a few months' time there will be fruit for the bats as well. ■

INDIAN SHORT-NOSED FRUIT BAT

feeding on bananas. The fiber of the fruit is sucked dry and then spat out on the ground.

KEY FACTS

● The throat opening in a fruit bat is so small that only the juice and tiny seeds are swallowed. The rest is spat out, thus spreading the seeds across the ground and regenerating the forest.

● All fruit bats forage for around two hours after sunset, and it is during this time that they acquire some 60–65 percent of their daily food requirement.

● During the dry seasons in the tropics, when fruit may be less available, fruit bats will often eat pollen and nectar instead.

NECTAR-EATING FRUIT BAT

As pollen rubs off on its body, the bat transfers it to other plants.

SOCIAL STRUCTURE

Very little is known about the social organization of fruit bats. Although they are often found in large groups, many species prefer to live in small groups numbering between 10 and 20 individuals.

The straw-colored fruit bat from Africa is one of the most gregarious examples and lives in colonies of up to one million individuals. However, these colonies are not completely stable. After the animals have mated in the period between April and

---

DOMINANT MALES ASSERT THEIR POSITION BY TAKING THE HIGHEST BRANCHES IN THE ROOSTING TREE

June, social bonds seem to break down and the colony disintegrates.

Female straw-colored fruit bats are unusual in that they can delay implanting the fertilized eggs into their uteri until September or October when a colony consisting mostly of females reassembles. This coincides with the start of the dry season. Their birth in either February or March coincides with the

beginning of the wet season, when food is most plentiful and their chances of survival are greater.

The epauletted bat from southwest Africa roosts in trees and remains alert throughout the day. These animals are not gregarious and are often found on their own or in groups consisting of two or three individuals.

The closely related epauletted fruit bat is more sociable. During the day, it roosts in groups of between 3 and 100 individuals of both sexes. When the breeding seasons are in progress, male epauletted fruit bats leave the colony and fly to nearby trees, where they begin calling and flashing their epaulettes. This display is designed to attract the females, and mating occurs soon afterward.

The short-nosed or dog-faced fruit bat of Southeast Asia lives in groups of six to twelve individuals, with the older males living separately. These are the only Old World bats that are known to build shelters, which they construct by biting out the middle fruit of the kitul palm. This leaves a hollow in the cluster of fruits in which the bats can shelter. ■

Indian flying foxes roosting during daylight. Social hierarchy determines their place in the tree.

E. & D. Hosking/FLPA

BATS GROOMING

This is a constant activity with bats. It keeps the fur clean and free of parasites.

All illustrations Barry Croucher/Wildlife Art Agency

CAVE-DWELLING FRUIT BAT

Not all fruit bats live in the trees. The exception is the rousette fruit bat, which lives in caves. It will also make its home in other sheltered spots, such as temples, tombs, and hollow tree trunks.

A possible adaptation for this confined and dark habitat is the development of a limited form of echolocation. As the rousette bat flies about in the dark, it makes a high-pitched buzzing sound that echoes off the walls, allowing it to judge distance. This bat does not possess the folds of skin that most small bats have, and neither does it have large, complex ears. However, its primitive radar seems sufficient for its needs.

147

REPRODUCTION

The time of year at which fruit bats mate varies greatly and will depend on the species. Because all fruit bats live in the tropics, they do not have to worry about winters and could mate several times a year, yet many of the larger species only mate once a year. For the tube-nosed fruit bats mating can take place at almost any time of the year, as the lush forests of the Solomon Islands remain fruitful all year round. The Indian flying fox, however, has a mating period that lasts from July to October. This means the young are born after the dry season. The hammer-headed fruit bat also mates during the dry season, and gives birth four months later.

MATING RITUALS

Mating rituals also vary widely. However, they are usually very noisy. The male gray-headed flying fox stakes a claim on the branch of the communal roost, but he may become so territorial that he will try to keep the entire tree to himself. Like most other fruit bats, he has an extra claw. This is used, along with his sharp canines, in disputes over roosting sites. Damage to the delicate wing membrane is not uncommon, but as it is well supplied

---

ALTHOUGH FRUIT BATS HAVE MATING RITUALS, ONCE THIS IS OVER, MALES HAVE NOTHING MORE TO DO WITH FEMALES

---

with blood vessels, the damage soon heals.

Once the male has laid his claim he waits until late afternoon, and as dusk falls he spreads his large wings and starts to flap them in a rhythmic way. At the same time he bares his teeth and makes short screechlike barks. As the male warms up, these get louder and more rapid. Eventually the females begin to move among the males. They will search for the bat with the biggest wings and the loudest screech. After mating the female will fly back to her own roost, while the male will remain where he is and try to attract more females. He will take no part in the rearing of the offspring.

Unlike the casual mating rituals of the gray-headed flying fox, the male hammer-headed fruit bat's courtship is highly structured. In hammer-headed fruit bat colonies the males assemble at sites called leks, where all the sexually mature males congregate. The lek is usually found alongside a stream or small river. Here between 30 and 150 mature males spread themselves out, with one

EMBRYONIC DEVELOPMENT

The development of the fetus in the bat's womb follows a similar pattern to other mammals, including humans.

The spinal cord and brain—the central nervous system—develop first, followed soon after, by the heart and somites (the early stages of muscle and bone). The limb buds develop early on, but the wing buds (the forelimbs) progress at a faster rate than the hind limbs.

Gestation lasts from 45 days for small bats to six months for larger species. Baby bats are born rear end first. This prevents their wings getting caught in the birth canal.

At birth, a baby fruit bat is at a fairly advanced stage in its physical development. It is roughly 30–40 percent of the size of an adult and is born well-haired and with its eyes open. Its wings are small, but its thumbs and hind feet are well developed, allowing the baby bat to grasp its mother's fur securely.

CENTRAL NERVOUS SYSTEM DEVELOPS

LIMB BUDS DEVELOP

All illustrations Kim Thompson

C. B. & D. W. Frith/Bruce Coleman Ltd.

(in) SIGHT

HAMMER-HEADED FRUIT BAT'S CALL

The hammer-headed fruit bat's cacophonous mating ritual is responsible for its distinctive looks. The male has a enormous bony larynx, or voice box, which fills most of its chest region and pushes all its other organs down into the stomach area. It has a funnel-shaped mouth, like a bullhorn, and large cheek pouches. The nasal cavity is also much enlarged, so that it acts as an acoustic amplifier. These features are all special adaptations that help produce the bat's loud call. They also give the hammer-headed fruit bat its characteristic hammer-shaped head.

Mother fruit bat with young (left). *The female is devoted to her young, leaving it near when foraging and locating it again through smell.*

Long tailed fruit bat suckling (right). *Soon after birth the young crawls to a nipple to suckle.*

FETUS NEARS TERM

WINGS BEGIN TO DEVELOP

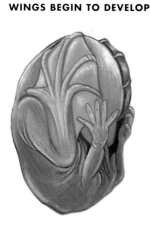

every 33 ft (10 m) or so. This happens twice a year, during the short and long dry seasons.

The mating ritual begins with the males making loud, monotonous honks 50–120 times a minute and flapping their wings furiously at twice their call rate. This attracts the females to the lek. Each female flies up and down the line of honking males until she spots a particularly impressive individual.

> TWIN BIRTHS ARE NOT UNCOMMON AMONG WELL-FED BATS, SO A GOOD FOOD SOURCE PROBABLY ENCOURAGES THIS

She hovers in front of him and examines him closely. The male increases the rate of his honking and wing flapping until it is a staccato buzz. The female will make several visits to the lek and hover in front of a number of males before suddenly landing on one. Mating lasts for 30 to 60 seconds, during which time the male falls silent. The female ends the mating with several squeals. She then flies off. Within a minute, the male begins his honking again in the hope of attracting another mate. Quite often it is only a handful of these males that mate, as the females are exceptionally choosy. ∎

LIFE CYCLE

The length of time it takes from mating to birth varies greatly; usually the smaller the animal, the shorter the amount of time. With fruit bats it can take over six months before the gestation period is complete, which is an incredibly long time for such relatively small animals—and it is even more incredible for an animal that relies on flight to obtain its food.

At birth a flying fox young is well developed. It is born fully furred and with its eyes open. In the Indian flying fox the newborn baby can weigh as much as 8.8 oz (250 g), almost one-third the adult female's own weight. Not surprisingly most flying foxes give birth to only a single offspring, although in the rousette fruit bat twins do occur. The newly born bat clings tightly to the mother and feeds from her breast at will. Despite the huge size of her baby,

---

SEXUAL MATURITY VARIES AMONG BAT SPECIES BUT CAN BE ANYWHERE FROM SIX MONTHS TO TWO YEARS

---

the female flying fox must carry her offspring with her on the nightly search for food. However, once the female has arrived at her feeding site, she will often unhook her young and leave it hanging from a nearby branch while she collects fruit.

For the Indian and gray flying foxes this will continue for two to three weeks. As it grows, the youngster rapidly becomes too heavy to carry, and the female will leave it behind, clinging to the tree. This is a dangerous time for the young flying fox, for if it should fall from the tree, it would become easy prey for any passing predators. On her return, after circling a few times, the mother locates her own offspring even though there may be hundreds

THE FIRST MOMENTS

A baby fruit bat is helpless and totally dependant on its mother at birth. It clings to its mother constantly until it is ready to fly. It can even feed while its mother is in flight, fastening on to her nipple with needlelike teeth. The females of some bat species have false teats that the baby bat can cling to when it is not feeding.

THE MATING GAME

The male bats mount females from behind, using wings and thumbs to hold the females still.

GUIDED BY SMELL

The fruit bat locates fruiting trees and then crushes the fruit for its juices.

All illustrations Evi Antoniou

GROWING UP

The life of a young fruit bat

BABY FRUIT BATS

They are born large, alert, and with their eyes open. This gives the bat a good chance of survival early on.

FROM BIRTH TO DEATH

INDIAN FLYING FOX
GESTATION: 140–160 DAYS
LITTER SIZE: 1
BREEDING: JULY–OCTOBER
WEIGHT AT BIRTH: 7–10 OZ (200–280 G)
EYES OPEN: AT BIRTH
FIRST FLIGHT: 2–3 MONTHS

WEANING: 5 MONTHS
INDEPENDENCE: 6–8 MONTHS
SEXUAL MATURITY: 18–24 MONTHS
LONGEVITY: USUALLY 12–15 YEARS IN THE WILD; UP TO 31 YEARS 5 MONTHS IN CAPTIVITY

ROUSETTE FRUIT BAT
GESTATION: 110–130 DAYS
LITTER SIZE: 1 (TWINS EVERY THIRD OR FOURTH YEAR)
BREEDING: JUNE–SEPTEMBER
WEIGHT AT BIRTH: 1–1.4 OZ (30–40 G)
EYES OPEN: AT BIRTH
FIRST FLIGHT: 4–5 MONTHS

WEANING 4 MONTHS
INDEPENDENCE: 5–6 MONTHS
SEXUAL MATURITY: 5 MONTHS FOR FEMALES; 15 MONTHS FOR MALES
LONGEVITY: USUALLY 11–14 YEARS IN THE WILD; UP TO 23 YEARS IN CAPTIVITY

BATS FORAGING

The mother cannot gather food and carry her young at the same time, so she leaves it hanging in branches.

of screaming infants all trying to gain attention. This is achieved through a combination of memory, eyesight, and hearing.

A young bat grows quickly, and it will only be another two to three months before it will be able to fly and begin to fend for itself. During the weeks before this happens, the young bat will hang upside down and flap its wings. This builds up its muscles. When it is ready, it simply lets go of its roost branch and drops. Unlike a bird, if it hits the ground it will be able to climb up a tree and try again. Yet even though the young bat is now able to fly, it will be nursed for another month or so by its mother and will remain with her for a further two to three months.

At about eight months old the young bat sets up a roost of its own. However, it will continue to grow until it is one year old. Young males will remain with their mothers until they are almost two years old before leaving to join the bottom rung of the hierarchy of the lek. ∎

FIRST FLIGHT

Larger fruit bat young take their first flight at three months. Even so, they continue to suckle.

FRUIT BAT FEUD

CAUGHT BETWEEN A DISAPPEARING HABITAT AND TEMPTING FRUIT
PLANTATIONS, FRUIT BATS FACE A BLEAK FUTURE AS THEY ARE FORCED
TO FEED ON FORBIDDEN FRUIT—AND FACE THE FARMERS' WRATH

Fruit bat numbers are declining throughout their range for many reasons. In the tropics, fruit bats are one of the most common mammals, especially on tropical forested islands. For thousands of years local people have hunted them and killed them for their meat.

This has been going on for so long that the human and fruit bat populations stabilized. The number of fruit bats that were killed and eaten

IN 1970 THERE WERE 3,000 MARIANAS FRUIT BATS. BY 1989 THERE WERE ONLY 400 TO 500 LEFT

were small compared with the population as a whole, so culling them had no serious effect. However, with better medical care, the human population of the islands is growing, and food is in short supply.

The local people had developed new and more effective techniques for capturing bats, such as stringing fishing nets between large trees on the bats' regular flight paths. Since World War II, the number of rifles has also increased, and the locals

IN 1991 VOLCANOES IN THE PHILIPPINES AND CYCLONES IN BANGLADESH DESTROYED BATS' HABITATS

use them for hunting. This has tipped the balance, and in many places the bat population is under severe pressure. On many isolated islands, as well as on the mainland, fruit bat populations are dwindling, and in some places bats are beginning to disappear altogether.

Unfortunately, fruit bats' problems do not stop

there. Their habitats are being destroyed, and in many places they are seen as pests. The growing humans populations of the developing regions where fruit bats are found need large amounts of tropical fruit, not just for local consumption but also for export. It is one of the few ways local people can earn foreign exchange. Commercial fruit farming requires the use of large tracts of land, and huge areas of unspoiled forest are being turned into plantations for crops such as banana, guava, dates, and other cash crops.

Such intensive farming can destroy the bats

The threatened Indian fruit bat in flight (right).
These bats are killed to make rheumatism lotion.

Stephen Dalton/NHPA

Belinda Wright/Oxford Scientific Films

Black flying foxes leaving their roost at sunset. Sadly,
they make an easy target for farmers and hunters.

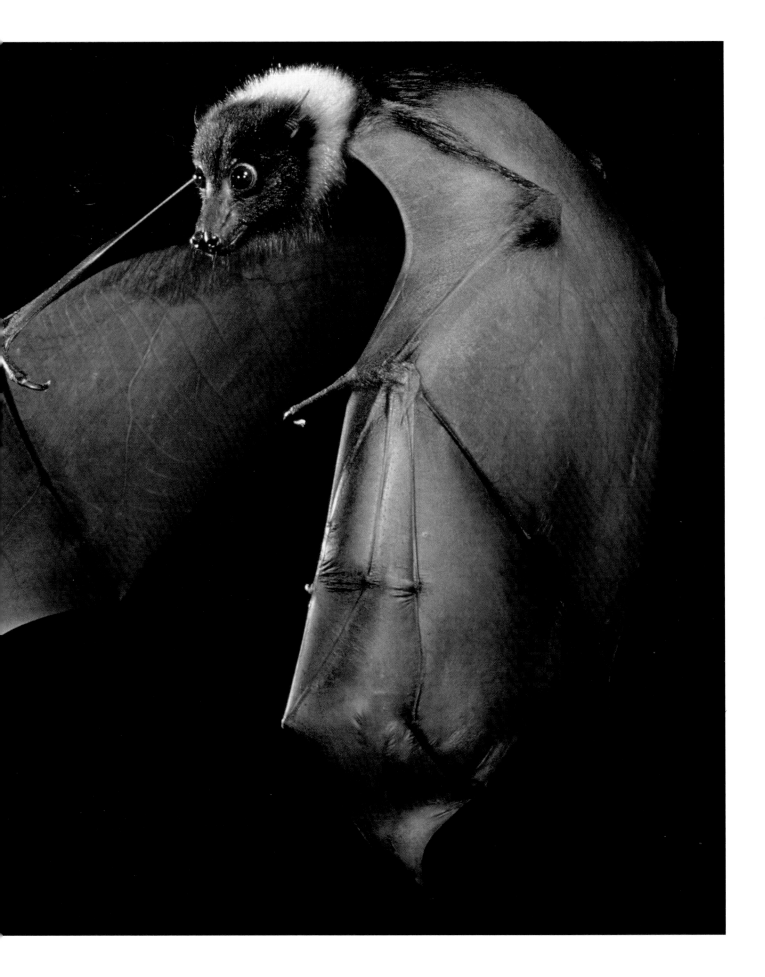

roosting trees which causes dangerous disruption. But, more important, planting fruit crops also brings the fruit bats into direct conflict with human beings and their livelihood.

Fruit bats will fly great distances to find food. When they discover these unnatural concentrations

---

IN CALIFORNIA, THE UNITED STATES AIR FORCE HAS MODIFIED ITS FLIGHT PATHS TO AVOID HITTING THE LOCAL BATS

---

of fruit-producing trees, huge numbers gather to feed. This feast only helps the fruit bats in the short term though. Their frenzied feeding can cause extensive damage, and the plantation owners take drastic and lethal action to protect their crops.

As plantations grew, humans and bats came increasingly into conflict. Initially, with the increased availability of fruit from the giant plantations, some bat populations actually grew. In Thailand fruit bats were said to destroy whole crops in a single night. But the local people could see their livelihood being eaten away, so they fought back very effectively—even a single blast from a shotgun can kill over 30 bats.

In Australia fruit bat populations declined rapidly after large numbers were poisoned to prevent them from damaging gardens and orchards. Soon the bats' future was in question. Several species, such as the Guam flying fox (*Pteropus tokudae*), have already become extinct, and many other species are on the verge of vanishing forever.

STUNTED TREES

There is little question that some fruit bats do cause extensive damage to these plantations. In Africa the widespread straw-colored flying fox not only eats vast quantities of the date harvest but also damages many of the young trees by gnawing the bark to get much-needed moisture during drier

---

NEWCASTLE VIRUS, DEADLY IN POULTRY, HAS BEEN SPREAD IN LATIN AMERICA TO EXTERMINATE BATS

---

seasons. Eventually this stunts the growth of the trees or even kills them.

However, the easy answer to the problem did not foresee the consequences. As numbers of fruit bats rapidly decreased, many valuable plants began to decline as well. In West Africa the straw-colored flying fox has been slaughtered in its thousands because it is considered to be a pest by humans. Only now are agriculturists realizing

David Woodfall/NHPA

ENDANGERED SPECIES

GUAM: THE EATER OF BATS

The island of Guam lies to the east of the Philippines and is the largest of a series of islands called the Marianas. Guam itself is small, with a population of some 130,000 people.

The flesh of the fruit bat has, for over 2,500 years, been considered a delicacy in the Marianas. Before travel between the islands of the western Pacific became as easy as it is today, the impact of humans on the bat population was minimal. However, that is not the case now. Modern killing methods, using fishing nets and shotguns, together with airplanes, fast boats, and even mobile freezer units, have tipped the balance against the bat.

Despite legal protection in several countries, Guam still manages to buy in at least 17,000 fruit bats a year, although the true figure is probably much higher.

The demand for bat flesh has caused dramatic population crashes in local bat species. Indeed, three extinct species came from this area alone. Unfortunately, the Marianas fruit bat is quite likely to join them, as its population in the wild dropped from over 3,000 in 1957 to less than 50 just 20 years later. Although the main population increased briefly in the first few years of the 1980s, it is thought

PICTURES OF EGYPTIAN ROUSETTE BATS *(RIGHT)* HAVE BEEN FOUND IN ANCIENT TOMBS.

CONSERVATION MEASURES

● Several specialist organizations have been set up to monitor wild populations of bats. Their aims are to stimulate interest within the countries where bats are found and to collect information about the bats' lifestyles and threats to their survival.

● Around the world there are several captive breeding programs. One of the most successful involved the Rodrigues flying fox, which numbered just 75 animals in 1974.

that these were bats that had been displaced from another island while trying to escape to safety.

A great fear is that as local species disappear, bats will be collected from areas farther afield. The island of Palau has been particularly hard hit. In the years between 1990 and 1992 over 20,000 fruit bats were collected from Palau alone, and the net is spreading. Already, bats from Papua New Guinea and Samoa are appearing in Guam.

Fortunately, this trade in fruit bats to Guam will probably decrease quite soon, as it is already becoming unpopular with the young. Unfortunately, this is not because of an awareness of the plight of these animals but because they feel that the smaller, imported bats do not have as much flavor, and are covered with external parasites such as fleas and lice.

Inset E. & D. Hosking/FLPA

- Zoologists in the United States are undertaking a major program to change the public image of bats. If the public's perception of bats was improved, many endangered species could be saved.

- Today conservationists are taking notice of the role bats play in regenerating the rain forest.

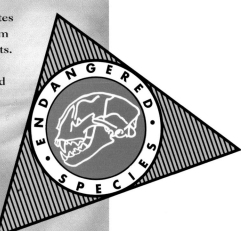

FRUIT BATS IN DANGER

TWO GENERA OF BATS ARE PROTECTED UNDER THE CONVENTION ON TRADE IN ENDANGERED SPECIES OF WILD FAUNA AND FLORA (CITES), THE FLYING FOX GENUS OF *PTEROPUS* AND THE SHARP-TOOTHED FRUIT BAT GENUS OF *ACERODON*. THIS COVERS 62 SPECIES OF FRUIT BAT. OF THESE, TRADE IS ILLEGAL IN THE FOLLOWING:

TRUK FLYING FOX	ENDANGERED
MORTLOCK FLYING FOX	ENDANGERED
MARIANAS FLYING FOX	ENDANGERED
PALAU FRUIT BAT	ENDANGERED
TONGAN FRUIT BAT	ENDANGERED

ENDANGERED MEANS THAT THE ANIMAL IS IN DANGER OF EXTINCTION, AND ITS SURVIVAL IS UNLIKELY UNLESS STEPS ARE TAKEN TO SAVE IT.

Hans Christian Heaps/Planet Earth Pictures

that the fruit bat is the main source of distribution of the seeds of the iroko tree, and growing iroko is one of the major local industries, bringing in over $230 million a year to West Africa.

On top of this, the fruit bats have to put up with the wholesale devastation of the forests. Throughout the tropics, huge areas of woodland are being destroyed both for the production of

---

BATS DIE BECAUSE THE CAVES, MINES, AND OLD DRAINAGE SYSTEMS THEY LIVE IN ARE BEING CLOSED FOR PUBLIC SAFETY

---

timber and for the building of farms. The huge pressures of burgeoning civilization and the growing population of these regions mean that more and more natural forest is being cleared to make room for roads and houses.

In the 1920s local populations of the common flying fox, the world's largest bat, were huge. In the Philippines, for example, single roosts boasting over 150,000 bats were not uncommon. Today even the largest colony of these impressive creatures may contain only around 400 members.

POLLINATION

Before humankind's growing population destroyed the delicate balance of most tropical ecosystems, fruit bats and indigenous trees existed in a perfect balance. Fruit bats play a vital part in the pollination

ALONGSIDE MAN

Churches and temples make perfect sanctuaries for bats. They roost in the rafters where it is dark and cool. They are especially lucky in southeast Asia, where the priests revere all life and tolerate the mess and noise the bats make. Short-faced fruit bats live in the temples of Thirupparankunram in southern India. And in the village of Pilingulum, 500 gigantic flying foxes live in a banyan tree which is now a shrine to the god Muni. Flying foxes are also protected for religious reasons in three other villages in the area—although generally in India they are classed as vermin and killed like rats and snakes.

Martin Dohrn/Bruce Coleman Ltd.

of the plants they feed from as they take pollen from plant to plant, in much the same way as bees. Once the fruits have formed, other bats eat the ripe fruit and distribute the seeds, either in their excrement or merely by dropping them after they have fed.

ROOSTING CAVES

Habitat destruction has also reduced bat populations and caused serious domino effects. In peninsula Malaysia, quarrying for lime destroyed the natural roosting caves of the dawn fruit bat (*Eonycteris pelaea*). Soon after this, the numbers of the much-prized durian fruit began to decline. Other reasons for the decline in the numbers of bats, however, are

rather more bizarre.

The Indian fruit bat had fared better than many species and, up until 20 to 30 years ago was not in any danger. However, it was believed locally that

ONE PLANTATION MANAGER IN NEW GUINEA ESTIMATED THAT BATS DESTROYED OVER $100 OF COCOA A MONTH

the bats' body fat could be turned into an ointment that would cure rheumatism. And the consequent mass culling of the Indian fruit bat to make rheumatism lotion has caused a serious drop in its numbers, especially in Pakistan. ■

Temples are built in the caves of southeast Bali where the revered rousette bats roost and breed.

As highways are cut through rain forests, bats' habitats are rapidly disappearing.

Morten Strange/NHPA

INTO THE FUTURE

The future survival of fruit bats is intrinsically linked with that of their habitat. As fruiting trees give way to grassland and houses, the bats can no longer find sources of food the whole year round. For mainland bats this can pose problems, but for those species that exist on islands, the results of deforestation can be devastating. As available habitat vanishes under the bulldozer, buffer zones that used to keep humans and bats apart are destroyed. Amazingly, some island species of fruit bat are still not afraid of humans and continue to fly about looking for food during the daytime, making themselves easy targets for shotguns.

Increased tourism has also adversely affected fruit bat populations. In addition to ending up on restaurant menus, many bats are killed flying into electricity and telephone wires.

At present there are only fifteen species of fruit bat on the IUCN Red Data List. The number is

PREDICTION
BACK FROM THE BRINK?

In 1948 in the Western Ghats of southern India a record was made of the observation of a rare bat called Salim Ali's. That was the last time it was seen until 1993, when it was discovered living on a coffee estate in the same region. Could it be that it is making a comeback?

almost certainly higher than this, but information is difficult to obtain. Of this number, however, three species are already thought to be extinct. In order to stop the trade in fruit bats, seven species have been placed under the protection of CITES (Convention on International Trade in Endangered Species of Wild Fauna and Flora). But it is almost impossible to patrol the fruit bats' entire range.

UNKNOWN THREATS

One of the biggest problems to be overcome in bat conservation is the lack of knowledge of how most species live and interact with the environment.

Many species live in relatively isolated locations, and the threats to their survival are many and varied—from disturbance by humans to natural disasters such as cyclones and droughts. Unfortunately bats do not fire the public's imagination as elephants and dolphins do. For this reason funding for projects is difficult to raise. ∎

Illustration Joanne Cowne

CAPTIVE BREEDING

As habitats are reduced or lost altogether, many species face extinction. One method used to avoid this is captive breeding. More and more wildlife parks and zoos are starting up programs to help threatened species build up numbers so that they can, at some point, be reintroduced into the wild. One fine example of how this can work is the saving of the Rodrigues fruit bat from Rodrigues Island, east of Mauritius.

Habitat destruction is not always caused by humans. In the tropics, powerful winds called cyclones occasionally sweep across the region. Just over 30 years ago, prior to a particularly violent cyclone, the Rodrigues fruit bat population was in a healthy state with over 2,000 individuals. After the cyclone had passed over the island, most of the fruit trees on which the bats fed were uprooted, and only 75 fruit bats were found alive. Slowly, numbers recovered until the population was up to 1,000. In the early 1990s, however, another cyclone hit, once again reducing the fruit bat numbers. However, Jersey Wildlife Preservation Trust started a breeding colony. Efforts were also made to replant trees and to protect those bats that remained. The captive colony is now thriving, with nearly 300 individuals. It is hoped that it will soon be possible to begin their reintroduction into the wild.

GUANO—FOOD FOR THOUGHT

Bats that use the same roosting sites for long periods of time, especially in caves, can provide an unexpected bonus for humans. After feeding, most bats return to the roost before their food is digested. Any excrement is allowed to drop to the floor.

After many years this excrement, or guano, builds up. It smells horrible but it is an excellent natural fertilizer as it contains large amounts of phosphorus, nitrogen, and potassium—all of which are essential to the healthy growth of plants.

LEAF-NOSED BATS

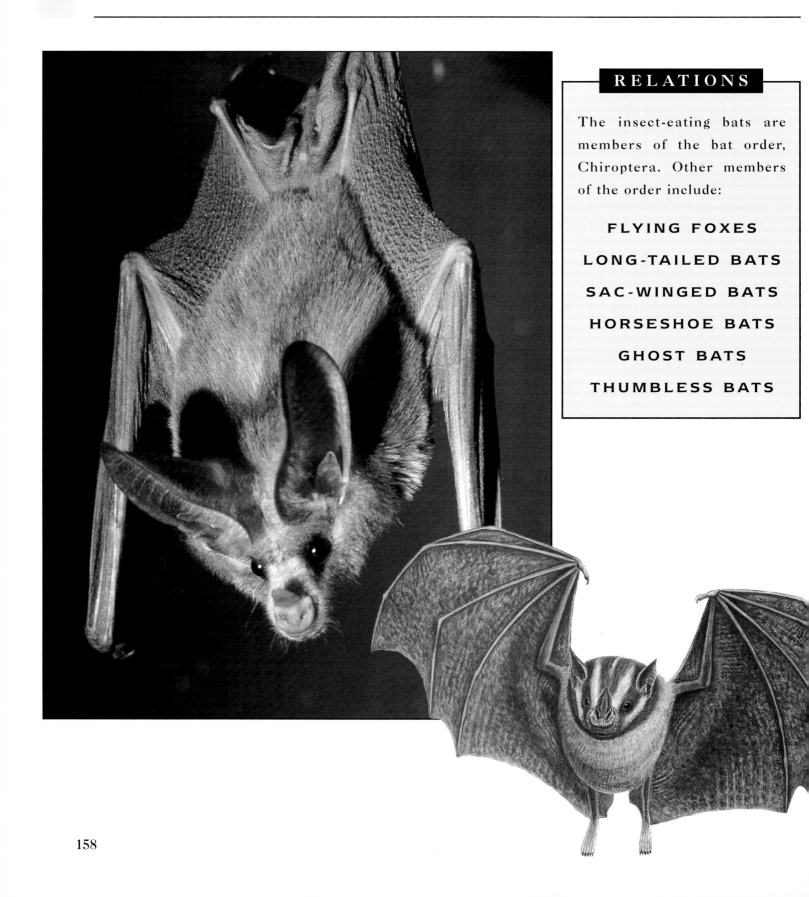

RELATIONS

The insect-eating bats are members of the bat order, Chiroptera. Other members of the order include:

FLYING FOXES

LONG-TAILED BATS

SAC-WINGED BATS

HORSESHOE BATS

GHOST BATS

THUMBLESS BATS

Merlin D. Tuttle/Photo Researchers Inc./OSF

WINGS IN THE NIGHT

UNIQUE AMONG MAMMALS IN THEIR ABILITY TO FLY, BATS HAVE ESTABLISHED THEMSELVES AS UNDISPUTED MASTERS OF THE NIGHT SKIES

B ats are one of the most numerous, diverse, and successful groups of mammals that have ever lived on earth. Over 950 species are known to exist— that's one-quarter of all present-day mammals—and zoologists are certain to discover more as natural wildernesses are more thoroughly explored. Bats have spread to almost every corner of the globe, from the fringes of the Arctic to the stormy southern tip of South America, and even to far-flung oceanic islands. The reasons for their success and adaptability lie in certain special features that make bats distinct from all other mammals.

The characteristic that, more than anything, makes a bat unmistakably a bat is its ability to fly. Some other mammals, including the so-called flying squirrels and flying lemurs, can glide from high to low on outstretched flaps of skin. But none can truly fly. Only the bat can take off and climb into the air, swoop and rise, hover, twist, and turn in an instant,

The world's bats are divided into two distinct groups: the insect-eating bats, or microbats (Microchiroptera), and the larger flying foxes, or megabats (Megachiroptera). The insect-eating bats consist of four superfamilies, which are further subdivided into eighteen families. The four families of bats featured in this article belong to the superfamily Phyllostomatoidea and comprise more than 160 species.

ORDER
Chiroptera
(bats)

SUBORDER
Microchiroptera
(insect-eating bats)

SUPERFAMILY
Phyllostomatoidea

LEAF-CHINNED BAT FAMILY
Mormoopidae

SHORT-TAILED BAT FAMILY
Mystacinidae

BULLDOG BAT FAMILY
Noctilionidae

LEAF-NOSED BAT FAMILY
Phyllostomidae

all the time powered by beats of its wings.

The bat's wings are, basically, greatly modified forelimbs; the skeletal structure, which consists of an upper arm, forearm, and five digits, follows the same basic pattern as other mammals. However, the upper arm bone is much shorter than the main forearm bone, and the finger bones are elongated.

THE MICROCHIROPTERA—OR SMALL BATS—ARE MOSTLY INSECT EATERS BUT INCLUDE SPECIES THAT EAT OTHER FOODS, INCLUDING BLOOD AND FRUIT

The wing membrane, or patagium (puht-AY-jee-um), extends from the back and belly; many bats have another, smaller membrane called the uropatagium, which extends between the hind limbs and tail. The patagium is the main flight surface; flapping is controlled by muscles connecting the breastbone, spine, and rib cage to the shoulder joints.

BIG HEARTED

Flying requires a plentiful supply of oxygen to the flight muscles, and the bat has special adaptations for this. Relative to its body size, a bat's heart is one of the largest of all mammals', and can pump out a high volume of oxygen-rich blood with each beat.

The development of flight in bats proved to be an enormously successful evolutionary step. It opened up new possibilities for finding food and gave bats the mobility to spread quickly into new areas. Flight enables an animal to forage more widely and

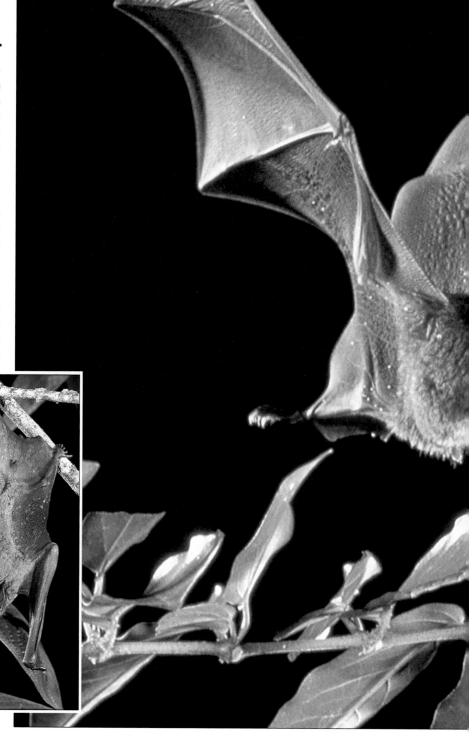

Active principally from dusk into the night, bats (such as the short-tailed fruit bat, far right) spend the day at rest. Because their forelimbs are so greatly modified, roosting bats (such as the greater spear-nosed bat, right) have to hang from their hind feet, with wings folded or furled. Yet they suffer no ill effects from long periods in an upside-down posture.

Merlin D. Tuttle/Bat Conservation International

Merlin D. Tuttle/Bat Conservation International

WHY BATS FLY

Merlin D. Tuttle/Bat Conservation International

Before bats evolved, birds ruled the skies. But though a few are active at night, birds mostly rely on sight and are limited to finding food by day. Since many insects, such as moths and beetles, had developed night-flying habits as a defense against birds, there was enormous potential in the air for any insect-eating animal that could sense movement in the dark. Bats quickly filled this vacant ecological role and were so successful that they diversified and could then take advantage of other food niches.

rapidly, an advantage when times are hard. It allows an animal to concentrate on one particular food source that may be highly nutritious but not always easy to find, such as ripe fruit. Flight also makes it easy to hunt and forage in the treetops, without being trapped there by tree-climbing enemies, and it gives bats the chance to pursue hordes of flying insects.

Bats are remarkable not just because they can fly with extreme agility but because they do so in the hours of darkness. Many mammals are nocturnal, but few share bats' ability to sense their surroundings in the dark with pinpoint accuracy.

THROUGH THE NIGHT

Though bats use sight and smell like other mammals, this is not enough to guide them through the night air in a crowded forest, avoiding obstacles and snatching flying insects. Instead, most bats navigate by echolocation, continuously emitting complex pulses of sound through their mouths or noses and listening for the pattern of echoes that return.

Though they share these basic characteristics,

bats have evolved a bewildering variety of habitat and food preferences, reflected in details of their physique and behavior. The leaf-chinned, bulldog, spear-nosed, and short-tailed bats—the group of four closely related bat families that make up the phyllostomatoid (FILL-oh-stom-a-toyed) superfamily and that are covered in this article—display better than any this sheer adaptability.

THESE FOUR BAT FAMILIES, THOUGH CLOSELY RELATED, SHOW GREAT VARIETY IN APPEARANCE AND BEHAVIOR

Here we have bats that fly either fast and direct or slowly and erratically; some that climb trees or hop across the ground. Many employ their skills to catch insects, but some hunt rodents, frogs, or fish, pluck fruit, sip nectar, or even feed on blood.

In the past these bats may have had a far wider distribution, but they have long disappeared from many areas. Indeed, the two short-tailed bats of New Zealand, one of which is almost certainly extinct, may well be approaching an evolutionary dead end.

NEW WORLD BATS
The other three families live in the New World, mostly in the tropical zones of forest and savanna, where they are abundant. Two of the families have only a handful of species: the leaf-chinned bats, which are mainly insectivorous and tend to roost in caves, and the bulldog bats, one of which is specialized for catching fish.

The remaining group, the leaf-nosed bats, is one of the largest of all bat families. It includes large carnivorous species, medium-sized fruit eaters and nectar feeders, and small insect eaters, as well as bats of varying sizes that enjoy a mixed diet.

COMMON BATS

Illustrations Kim Thompson

THE BATS' FAMILY TREE

Scientists have had difficulties in working out the relationships among the various bat species, partly because many of them have been poorly studied, and new research is always likely to suggest new groupings or regroupings. For many years there were thought to be five different families making up the phyllostomatoid superfamily, but recent comparisons of body structure and genetics have led zoologists to the conclusion that the vampire bat and its close relations, formerly thought to be a separate family called Desmodontidae, are in fact members of Phyllostomidae.

LEAF-CHINNED BATS
Mormoopidae (more-mo-OP-id-eye)

This family contains eight species; Peters's ghost-faced bat (Mormoops megalophylla [more-MO-ops meg-al-o-FILL-ah]) is shown at right.
Other species in the family include the naked-backed, ghost-faced, and mustached bats; these bats have basic nose leaves and a funnel-shaped mouth with a mustache near the end of the muzzle.

SHORT-TAILED BATS
Mystacinidae (mist-uh-SEEN-id-eye)

There is one genus with two species (one probably extinct). The New Zealand short-tailed bat, or Mystacina tuberculata (mist-uh-SEEN-uh too-ber-kyoo-LAH-ta), is shown above. These **bats have long muzzles and dense fur, and the claws on thumbs and toes have an extra small projection. Their wings fold in a unique manner: They lie close to the bat's body and out of the way.**

EARLY INSEC

LEAF-NOSED BATS
Phyllostomidae (fill-o-STOM-id-eye)

There are 50 genera containing approximately 150 species; the common vampire bat, or *Desmodus rotundus* (des-MODE-us ro-TUN-duss), is shown at right.

Most of the bats in this large family have fairly simple, spear-shaped nose leaves; in some they are very basic. Phyllostomid bats generally have simple ears. Tail length and fur color vary considerably; some species have striped fur.

FLYING FOXES

Bruce Coleman Ltd.

About 175 species of flying foxes make up the suborder Megachiroptera. They are large, fruit-eating bats that get their name from their foxlike faces and that inhabit the tropics of the Old World.

Because the fossil record is very poor, no one is sure whether the two bat suborders have a common ancestor. Some zoologists, pointing to the number of characteristics the flying foxes share with the primates, believe the suborders evolved separately. Genetic studies suggest otherwise.

BULLDOG BATS
Noctilionidae (nok-til-ee-ON-id-eye)

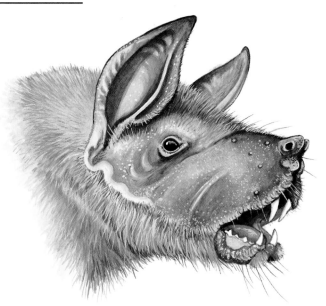

This family contains one genus with two species. *Noctilio leporinus* (nok-TIL-ee-oh lep-or-EE-nus)—known as the greater bulldog bat or fishing bulldog bat—is shown above.

The two species of bulldog bat have swollen lips, large ears, and a distinctive build, with broad tails, long hind legs, and large hind feet. Their long, narrow wings reach only to the knee (most bats' wings reach as far as the ankle).

HORSESHOE BATS

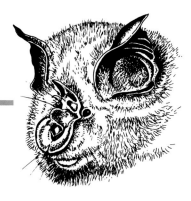

SHEATH-TAILED BATS

...ATING BATS

ANATOMY:
THE VAMPIRE BAT

THE WING MEMBRANE

consists of a double layer of skin enclosing muscles and elastic fibers. These control its stiffness, making it taut for flight but relaxed and easy to roll up when not in use.

THE FUR

or pelage of cave-dwelling bats such as the vampire is quite short, but species that roost in more exposed sites have longer fur for better insulation against cold winds and rain.

EARS

are large, complex, and folded. They are used to receive the vibrations that help the bat to find its prey.

The vampire (top) is, perhaps, much smaller than people think: With wings folded, it can easily fit into the palm of a hand. Its wingspan averages 8 in (20 cm), while that of the bulldog bat (bottom) measures about 11.5 in (29 cm).

COZUMEL SPEAR-NOSED BAT

TOME'S LONG-EARED BAT

Bats have a variety of outgrowths from their snout or lips, which may take the form of lance-shaped projections or strange flaps of skin (left). These nose leaves are used to modify or focus the echolocation calls that bats emit. The bizarre wrinkle-faced bat has, as well as a nose leaf, a fold of skin on its chin that acts as a kind of mask when it is extended upward, covering the bat's face when it is roosting.

SEBA'S SHORT-TAILED BAT

WRINKLE-FACED BAT

THE FLAT FACE

and short, broad snout of the vampire bat enable it to sink its teeth into its prey. Its eyes are relatively large but, probably, unable to perceive colors.

 Illustrations John Cox/Wildlife Art Agency

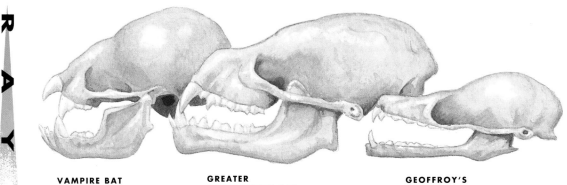

The greater spear-nosed bat, which has a broad diet that includes small vertebrates, insects, and fruit, has a strong skull and generalized teeth that can be used for crushing or grinding. Geoffroy's long-nosed bat has a more delicate skull and poorly developed

VAMPIRE BAT

GREATER SPEAR-NOSED BAT

GEOFFROY'S LONG-NOSED BAT

X-ray illustrations Elisabeth Smith

THE COMMON VAMPIRE BAT

CLASSIFICATION

GENUS: *DESMODUS*

SPECIES: *ROTUNDUS*

SIZE

HEAD–BODY LENGTH: 3–3.5 IN (70–90 MM)

WEIGHT/MALE: 0.5–2 oz (15–50 G)

WINGSPAN: 6.5–10 IN (160–250 MM)

WEIGHT AT BIRTH: 0.25 OZ (5–7 G)

COLORATION

DARK GRAY/BROWN ON UPPER PARTS, PALER (OFTEN WHITISH OR BUFF) ON THE UNDERSIDE

YOUNG: PINK

FEATURES

DARK BROWN EYES

FORWARD-FACING, POINTED EARS

ENLARGED, RAZOR-SHARP UPPER INCISOR AND CANINE TEETH

LONG, GROOVED TONGUE

SHORT, NAKED SNOUT WITH PROMINENT GROOVES

TOME'S LONG-EARED BAT

SHORT-FACED BAT

VAMPIRE BAT

BULLDOG BAT

All bats have a large ear flap called the pinna, and some insect-eating bats have a tragus, or earlet—a smaller projection made of cartilage—in front. The size and shape of the tragus vary considerably among the species.

pinna

tragus

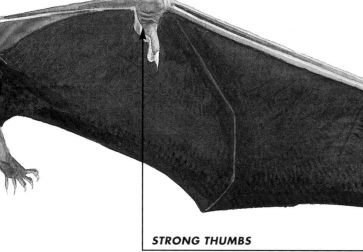

THE FINGER BONES

are enormously elongated to support the wing membrane; the length of the bones varies, though, from one family to another.

STRONG THUMBS

Vampires have strong, hook-shaped thumbs that they use to pull themselves forward when they crawl and that provide thrust when they hop or jump.

---

teeth. It has little need for powerful jaws or strong teeth, as it feeds primarily on nectar and pollen. The vampire bat, by contrast, has a strong jaw for biting into flesh and a short but broad snout, making room for enlarged and highly specialized teeth.

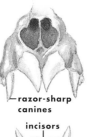

razor-sharp canines

incisors

VAMPIRE BAT

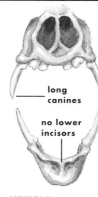

long canines

no lower incisors

MEXICAN LONG-TONGUED BAT

The vampire's upper canines and incisors are sharp for slicing through skin; its cheek teeth have few crushing surfaces, since it subsists on a liquid diet.

The Mexican long-tongued bat extracts nectar by extending its tongue into flowers. It has no lower incisors, which means it has less chance of biting its tongue.

STOMACH

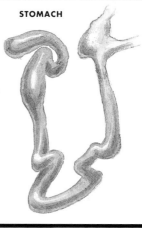

The stomach of the vampire bat is built to allow the animal to take in large quantities of blood quickly. One end of the tubular stomach is folded into a U shape that can swell up to four times in diameter and expand in length when the bat feeds.

BATS IN ABUNDANCE

THE TROPICAL WORLD PROVIDES A WIDE RANGE OF HABITATS AND FOOD SOURCES, AND BATS HAVE EVOLVED ALL MANNER OF LIFESTYLES IN ORDER TO EXPLOIT THE DIVERSITY OF NICHES AVAILABLE

The phyllostomatoid bats have evolved a bewildering variety of feeding tastes and foraging styles, preferences for different habitats and patterns of social life. Such varied behavior is fully in keeping with the wide range of ecological niches presented by tropical environments and the abundant opportunities opened up to bats by flight. Even so, all of them share traits common to bats worldwide.

TWILIGHT WORLD

Most important, bats are nocturnal creatures. Though some may begin their activity during the day, particularly toward twilight, bats are primarily nighttime feeders, resting during the day in concealed roosting sites. Because most bats are not very agile, it is vital for them to seek roosting sites in

---

THE NIGHTTIME IS THE RIGHT TIME FOR BATS: HUNTING, FEEDING, MATING—ALL TAKE PLACE AFTER DARK

---

which they are hidden but from which they can readily escape. If cornered and unable to fly, bats are easy prey for predators such as snakes and other carnivorous animals.

While bats are at rest, their heart rate falls to about one half of that during flight. The typical resting position is to hang upside down from the hind feet, with wings folded. The strong hind claws grip bark, stems, and cracks in rock; sometimes bats wedge their bodies into vertical fissures.

Roosts are not only places to rest; they are also homes to bats and the places where they spend most of their lives. They act as refuges from adverse weather and are the sites of most social interactions and the places where bats mate and rear their young.

Rather than a quiet place of rest, a large roost is usually a bustling pandemonium, with bats jostling for position, nursing infants, and grooming fur with tongue and hind claw while hanging from one leg.

TROPICAL HEAT

In the heat of the tropics, roosting bats need to shift position repeatedly to find cooler spots, under more shade or further from a cave entrance. Sometimes they move by shuffling their feet or by using their

Merlin D. Tuttle/Bat Conservation International

One of the most abundant species in Latin America, short-tailed spear-nosed bats (left) forage for a wide variety of energy-rich fruits, which they consume on a feeding perch.

Merlin D. Tuttle/Bat Conservation International

Ken Lucas/Planet Earth Pictures

The large roosts of vampire bats (above), *populated by relatives and neighbors, provide a strong support network. Tent-making bats* (inset), *on the other hand, live in small roosts and forage alone.*

thumb claws to clamber around. Otherwise they simply flutter to a new spot.

When in large numbers, many bats, such as the leaf-chinned bats, roost in scattered fashion rather than in a single massed colony. Other species gather in dense crowds, perhaps because they have greater social cohesion or because they choose the defensive strategy of safety in numbers. Constant jostling in such tight aggregations becomes more energetic as evening approaches, until the restless colony finally departs to feed, emerging from its roost in a spectacular swirl of wings.

The timing and duration of feeding flights vary from species to species. Bulldog bats may emerge from their roosts as early as late afternoon, while most other bats become active around sunset.

UNDER COVER

Vampire bats, on the other hand, prefer to hunt under cover of complete darkness and are much less active in moonlit hours. Since they have to disperse far and wide to find enough food for all, colonial species, such as long-nosed bats, tend to fly furthest to reach their feeding sites. ∎

HABITATS

These Honduran white bats are known as tent-making bats, as they roost beneath palm leaves, which they bite into a wedge shape.

Phyllostomatoid bats occur throughout a wide range of habitats. Though the lesser short-tailed bat is more or less restricted to a few forests in New Zealand, the other species range across varied terrain, from the arid lands of the southwestern United States through the tropical forests of the Caribbean and South America to the subtropical grasslands, or pampas, of southern Brazil and northern Argentina.

HERE, THERE, EVERYWHERE
Some species, such as bulldog bats, may be seen over coastal lagoons and mangrove swamps; others are a common sight in built-up areas, where they may hawk for flying insects attracted to streetlights.

Many bat species, such as the greater spear-nosed bat, occur in both open and densely wooded terrain, but others have more distinct habitat preferences linked to their particular diets.

Fruit-eating bats are likely to occur in tropical forests, where the variety of fruiting trees is high,

DISTRIBUTION

The Phyllostomidae number among the largest of bat families, with about 150 different species. They are found only in the tropical and subtropical areas of the New World. The Noctilionidae, while covering the same area, are limited to only two species, including the famous fishing bat.

KEY

■ PHYLLOSTOMIDAE

▨ NOCTILIONIDAE

Dieter & Mary Plage/Survival Anglia

FOCUS ON

CAVES
Few animals are as closely associated with caves as bats. With their ability to fly through deep tunnels in darkness, bats are perfectly at home in places forbidding to most other creatures. Caves provide them with secure, spacious sites, unexposed to wind and rain, in which they can roost, rear their young and, in the case of temperate species, hibernate, with minimum disturbance from other wildlife.

MASSIVE COLONIES
Bats can congregate in caves in large numbers, sometimes crowded to the roof in concentrations of more than a thousand to the square yard; the biggest colonies are numbered in millions. Many caves in the West Indies and Central and South America are colonized by several species. Tamana Cave on the Caribbean island of Trinidad, for example, is home to twelve different bats, and one cavern in Sinalao, Mexico, houses five of the eight recognized species of leaf-chinned bats.

Different species tend to occupy different parts of a cave. For example, the big-eared bat, a member of the leaf-nosed bat family, tolerates some light and is often found as close as 6 feet (2 meters) to the cave entrance. In contrast, mustached bats, members of the leaf-chinned bat family, prefer dark recesses.

NEIGHBORS

Tropical caves are home not just to bat colonies but also to other highly specialized creatures that have evolved to deal with the particular problems of life in the constant darkness.

CAVE FISH

With no need for sight, this small, strange fish has no eyes. Instead, it navigates using its sensitive fins.

though they are also found near plantations.

Insect-eating bats tend to concentrate in humid areas, often along rivers and over swamps where the flying insects are concentrated. The fishing bulldog bat and the fringe-lipped bat, which preys heavily on frogs, naturally prefer to hunt over water.

Whether bats inhabit a particular area also depends on the availability of safe roosting sites.

Stephen J. Krasemann/Bruce Coleman Ltd.

Illustrations Peter Bull

OILBIRD

Oilbirds nest deep inside caves and, like bats, use echolocation to guide them to and from the entrance.

CENTIPEDE

Centipedes up to 8 in (20 cm) in length patrol tropical caves, lying in wait for crickets and other insects.

Exclusively cave-dwelling species, such as the leaf-chinned bats, depend on geological formations such as limestone hills or coastal cliffs.

Many species of bat are not limited to caves; some prefer alternative hideaways such as tree cavities, termite nests, and rock fissures. Abandoned houses on cattle ranches are increasingly likely havens for common vampire bats. ∎

INSIDE THE BATS' CAVE

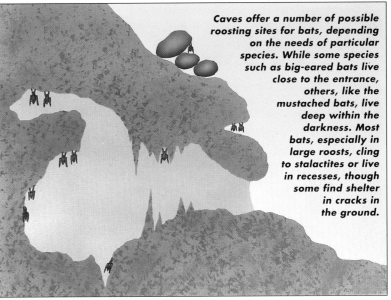

Caves offer a number of possible roosting sites for bats, depending on the needs of particular species. While some species such as big-eared bats live close to the entrance, others, like the mustached bats, live deep within the darkness. Most bats, especially in large roosts, cling to stalactites or live in recesses, though some find shelter in cracks in the ground.

Illustration Mark Franklin

FOOD AND FEEDING

The range of habitats occupied by Latin American bats is paralleled by their equally diverse array of food sources. Some species are generalists, able to eat a wide range of both animal and plant foods, while others are much more specialized. Items eaten include insects, fish, frogs, lizards, small birds and mammals, a wide range of fruit, and the nectar and pollen from flowers.

The widespread vegetarian habits of roughly one-third of these New World bats give them the same ecological role as that of the flying foxes in the Old World. Hundreds of plant species rely on bats for pollination and seed dispersal, including the kapok, one of the biggest of all rain forest trees.

Bat-pollinated plants tend to produce large, pale-petaled flowers that open in the evening. The

> AS THE BATS FEED ON NECTAR, LARGE AMOUNTS OF POLLEN ARE DUSTED ONTO THEIR HEADS, READY TO BE TRANSFERRED TO OTHER FLOWERS

blooms show up well in the dark and have a musky scent, so they will attract nectar-feeding bats that rely on sight and smell rather than sound to locate their food. The flowers may sprout directly from the plant stem or trunk or hang on drooping projections, allowing bats to reach them easily by hovering or perching nearby.

Fruit-eating bats help the spread of forest trees by swallowing fruit and depositing the seeds elsewhere in their droppings. They are especially fond of small fruits such as figs and the flesh surrounding nuts. They generally pluck fruit from the plant and carry it to a safe perch or back to their roost to eat. Food passes through the gut, where the nutritious parts are absorbed, in less than 20 minutes; digestion is so quick that the seeds and nuts are rarely damaged.

PROBING FOR NECTAR

The feeding habits of the Mexican long-nosed bat, a leaf-nosed bat that dwells in dry, open habitats, have been closely studied. This bat consumes nectar, pollen, and fruit and, like many nectar-feeding bats, it has a long snout and a very long tongue that can extend up to 3 inches (7.5 cm) from its mouth. These enable it to probe into flowers while flying slowly above them. Fleshy projections on the tip of its tongue help it to pick up the nectar and pollen within.

The blooms of desert cacti and agaves are vital to its diet. It may also feed on cactus fruit, probing among the spines and biting through the skin before inserting its tongue into the fruit pulp to lap up the juices.

Bats often congregate at good

Illustration Dan Wright

FRUITFUL MIGRATION

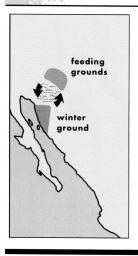

feeding grounds

winter ground

Some long-nosed bat populations migrate from winter grounds in Mexico through the Sonoran Desert to summer feeding grounds in Arizona. The same locality tends to be used year after year, and the bats are important pollinators for the agave and saguaro cacti in the region.

DESERT BLOOM

With the aid of its huge tongue, covered with sticky, bristlelike projections, a Mexican long-nosed bat takes its turn to feed on the colorful, nectar-rich blossoms of a blooming desert cactus.

feeding sites, but normally they will do so as competing individuals. Groups of about 25 Mexican long-nosed bats, on the other hand, have been seen to form cohesive flocks, each of which moves as a unit from plant to plant.

COLLECTIVE ACTION

The key advantage of this strategy is that the flock can pool the knowledge gained by a number of bats as they make preliminary searching forays. The desert blooms on which they feed are patchily distributed, and one individual bat could waste much effort searching for food on its own. It saves vital energy if the bats share knowledge of, and access to, a wide range of food sources.

Stephen Krasemann/NHPA

Members of the flock, which generally consists of females and their recent young, circle together over a plant and take turns flying down and making a passing visit to a flower or two.

After a while, individual bats will increasingly find that the flowers they visit have already been depleted of nectar and their turn is unsuccessful. Even so, the circling pattern is maintained and there is little of the aggression that might be expected from other bats competing at a scarce food source. After several minutes of feeding at a site found by one bat, it is usual for a different individual to move to another site that it has previously investigated. The whole flock will immediately follow. ■

A flock of longed-nosed bats (above) *sets out on its way to another communal feeding site.*

Like stacked airplanes seeking permission to land (right), *long-nosed bats line up patiently for their turn at feeding.*

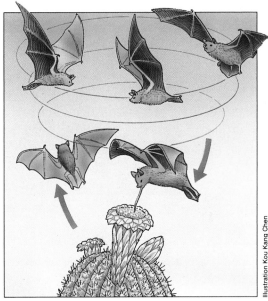

Illustration Kou Kang Chen

AMAZING FACTS

FINE JUDGMENT

Recent research involving computer simulation suggests that flocks of Mexican long-nosed bats make an incredibly accurate judgment of when to change feeding sites.

When one bat takes the initiative to switch sites, it generally coincides with a critical point when so many of the flowers have been depleted of nectar that it would be more beneficial in energy terms to move on to another site where the flowers are full rather than to search for the remaining nectar.

Such powers of judgment may be vital to the bats' survival in a desert environment, which leaves little room for error.

Illustration Dan Wright

HUNTING

The vampire has fewer teeth than any other bat species; its liquid diet means that only its razor-sharp incisors are of vital importance.

The feeding habits of vampire bats have made them notorious far beyond their geographical range. The three species apparently subsist exclusively on fresh blood. Two of them, the white-winged and the hairy-legged vampire bats, prefer to consume the blood of birds, especially domestic chickens. But the third, the common vampire, attacks cattle, pigs, goats, horses, asses, and, occasionally, humans. It is this species that has been most closely studied.

The common vampire consumes almost one fluid ounce (up to 20 ml) of blood per night. It feeds by stealth, under the cover of complete darkness and, unless disturbed, will drink its fill from a single sleeping victim.

Its usual method of attack is to alight on the ground close to a resting animal and locate a suitable site for biting. Often this will be a patch of bare or lightly furred skin above the hooves, around the anal or genital areas, on the nostrils and lips, or on the ears. The bat may have to climb onto the victim to reach a suitable site, but it is so light that a large animal may well fail to notice as the bat bites a small, neat hole through the skin.

> AFTER SELECTING A SUITABLE VICTIM, A VAMPIRE BAT MAY GORGE ITSELF ON ITS OWN BODY WEIGHT IN BLOOD, MAKING IT DIFFICULT TO FLY AWAY

Blood from the wound is directed into the bat's mouth via its tongue, and anticoagulants in the saliva prevent the wound from clotting until after the bat has completed its meal, which may take up to twenty minutes.

The common vampire bat is believed to locate its prey in the gloom largely by a combination of sight and sound, rather than by echolocation. It flies low and silently over the ground, often following known

THE DANCE OF THE VAMPIRE
Vampires feed on animals that may be up to 10,000 times their own body weight and that congregate in large herds. This calls for a cautious and stealthy approach, in which the bat appears to dance toward its victim.

HOPPING
from its hind legs onto its wrists, the vampire moves delicately toward its prey, careful not to rouse the intended "blood donor" or its neighbors.

PREY

The domesticated cattle brought to South and Central America by the Spanish invaders dramatically increased the food options available to the vampire bat. Wild animals such as the tapir are attacked much less often.

TAPIR

ZEBU CATTLE

BROWN SWISS CATTLE

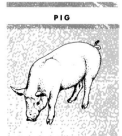
PIG

flight routes such as rivers to navigate from its roost sites to areas cattle frequent. The bat then selects the most appropriate victim from the herd.

An animal lying down is preferable, since it is less likely to deter the bat and there is less chance that the bat might be crushed underfoot if the animal moves abruptly. For the same reasons it is better for the bat to choose a victim on the periphery of the herd than one among others.

LIKELY VICTIMS

According to such criteria, certain individuals in a cattle herd are more likely to be bitten by vampire bats than others. Calves are vulnerable and often have wounds in various states of healing because they tend to spend more time lying down than adult cattle, and because cows with calves tend to space themselves apart from other cattle. Cows in heat also tend to settle on the outside of the herd, and are therefore bitten more often.

A study of a mixed herd of zebu and brown Swiss cattle in Costa Rica showed that the brown Swiss had more bite wounds on average, as they settled less often in the center of the herd, where the tight cluster gave good protection from attack.

Stephen Dalton/OSF

A NIMBLE APPROACH

Vampire bats are very agile, climbing in roosts and moving across the ground to approach their prey. As they shuffle rapidly forward, they can be mistaken for true four-legged animals, propped up behind on their strong hind legs and toes and supported in front by their long thumbs and the wrists of their furled wings.

The common vampire can hop forward, pivoting on its forelimbs, and leap up to 6 inches (15 cm) clear of the ground. This is enough space for it to manage one downbeat of its wings and lift itself into flight.

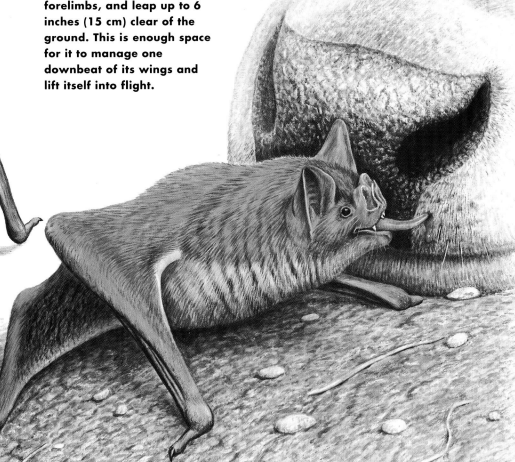

AFTER SHAVING
a patch on its victim, the vampire bites. The bat's saliva inhibits clotting and allows the creature to lap up the blood of its prey with its grooved tongue.

Most of the hunting bats rely on insects for the bulk of their prey, employing two principal methods to catch them. The method for which bats are best known is the capture of insects on the wing using echolocation as a guide; the other is foraging.

The leaf-chinned bats are the acknowledged masters of aerial pursuit. Their open mouths form funnels surrounded by stiff hairs that direct the airflow inward, helping the bats scoop up flying insects as they pass.

Many bats catch nonflying insects by homing in on them and picking them from leaves, bark, and even off the ground—a method referred to as gleaning. Some bats will even perch to catch prey. Peters's spear-nosed bat has been known to raid the nests of wasps to eat their larvae and pupae.

ON THE FLOOR

The bat that is most remarkable for its nonaerial foraging is, perhaps, the short-tailed bat. Though it can hunt on the wing, it prefers to scuttle over debris on the forest floor and across branches, snatching insects and other invertebrates. When its wings are tightly folded, they become equivalent to normal forelimbs, making walking, climbing, and even running easy.

At least four species of leaf-nosed bats are thought to be carnivorous, feeding when they can on small vertebrates. The fringe-lipped bat has become an expert predator of frogs, homing in on their courtship calls and snatching them as they sit half-exposed in the shallows of marshes and pools. This species also gleans small lizards such as geckos from foliage and branches, a trait shared by the greater spear-nosed bat.

THE BULLDOG BAT, *having located its prey, swoops down near the surface of the water. It folds its tail membrane out of the way, trails its feet through the water, and impales the victim with its deadly talons. The bat can reach as much as 1 inch (3 centimeters) below the water when flying.*

The giants among the carnivorous bats are the two species of so-called false vampires, one of which has a wingspan of up to 3.3 feet (1 meter) and is the biggest bat in the Americas. False vampires have powerful jaws and large canine teeth for dealing with prey such as small birds, rodents, and even other bats, including the greater spear-nosed bat. A false vampire may hunt from a lookout post, rather like a bird of prey, and then swoop to pounce on its victim. It typically kills the prey with a bite

AFTER STRIKING *successfully, the bat rises from the surface, water draining easily from its short coat. While flying, it transfers the prey to its mouth, where it is held by sharp canine teeth and wedged into the bat's flexible cheeks.*

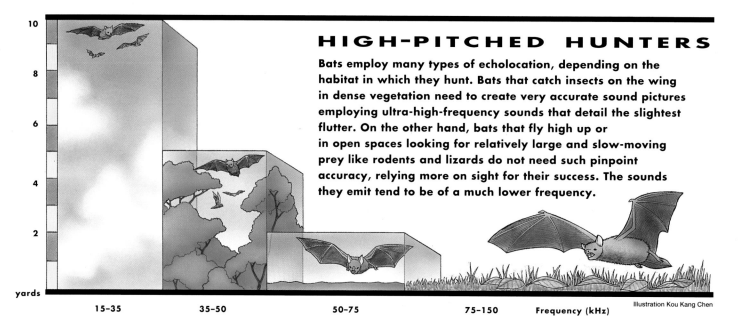

HIGH-PITCHED HUNTERS

Bats employ many types of echolocation, depending on the habitat in which they hunt. Bats that catch insects on the wing in dense vegetation need to create very accurate sound pictures employing ultra-high-frequency sounds that detail the slightest flutter. On the other hand, bats that fly high up or in open spaces looking for relatively large and slow-moving prey like rodents and lizards do not need such pinpoint accuracy, relying more on sight for their success. The sounds they emit tend to be of a much lower frequency.

yards				
15–35	35–50	50–75	75–150	Frequency (kHz)

Illustration Kou Kang Chen

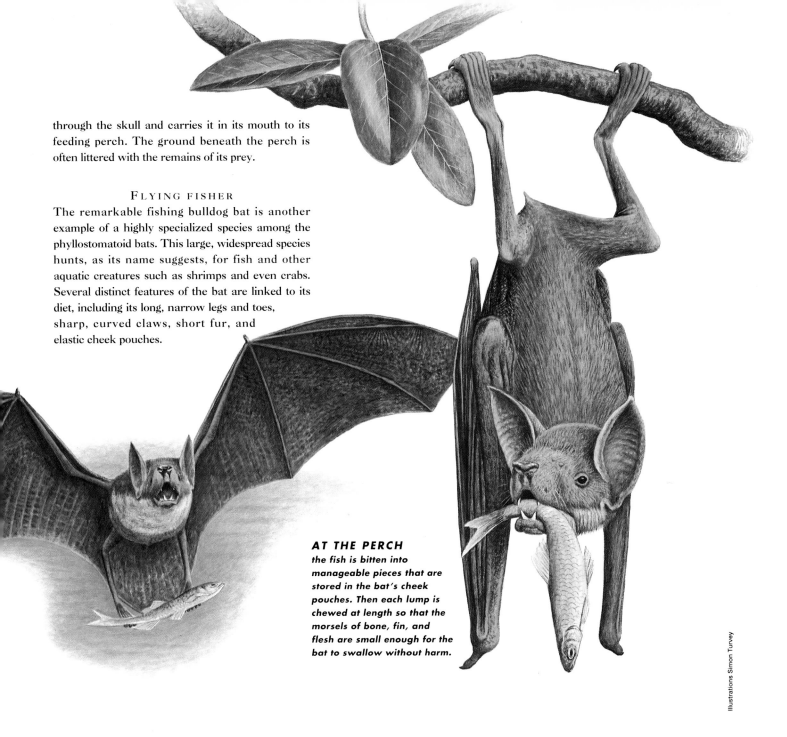

through the skull and carries it in its mouth to its feeding perch. The ground beneath the perch is often littered with the remains of its prey.

FLYING FISHER

The remarkable fishing bulldog bat is another example of a highly specialized species among the phyllostomatoid bats. This large, widespread species hunts, as its name suggests, for fish and other aquatic creatures such as shrimps and even crabs. Several distinct features of the bat are linked to its diet, including its long, narrow legs and toes, sharp, curved claws, short fur, and elastic cheek pouches.

AT THE PERCH
the fish is bitten into manageable pieces that are stored in the bat's cheek pouches. Then each lump is chewed at length so that the morsels of bone, fin, and flesh are small enough for the bat to swallow without harm.

Illustrations Simon Turvey

The bulldog bat hunts over rivers, ponds, lagoons, and even over the sea, making slow zigzag flights. As it does so, it listens to the echo of its sound pulses and seems able to detect reflections from the ripples produced by fish breaking the surface of the water.

CRASH-LANDING

The bat usually sweeps down on its intended victim, dragging its sharp claws in the water. It hooks the fish and then flies off to consume its prey, though, if necessary, the bat can crash-land on the surface and make swimming strokes with its wings. As many as 30 fish may be consumed in a single night. The bulldog bat has been known to feed among pelicans, swooping down to snatch fish either disturbed or wounded by the birds' lunges. ∎

FINE TUNING

Parnell's mustached bats, which forage in areas of thick vegetation in northern South America, Central America, and the West Indies, are the only bats in the New World with the ability to detect fluttering insects. The bats' finely tuned hearing system locates their own calls as they echo back from flying insects, allowing the bats to gauge accurately the prey's position.

Merlin D. Tuttle/Bat Conservation International

LIFE CYCLE

Phyllostomatoid bats, unlike bats that live in temperate climates, are not tied to distinct breeding seasons, as food levels in the tropics do not fluctuate much during the year. The Cuban flower bat breeds at any time, and Pallas's long-tongued bat may give birth two or three times a year. Nevertheless, some species have breeding peaks, resulting in more young being born at certain times of the year. Studies of the Jamaican fruit-eating bat in Panama have shown birth peaks from March to April and from July to August.

Courtship between bats usually takes place at roosting sites, and bats are able to mate while hanging upside down. In most species it is the female who is responsible for rearing the young, but some leaf-nosed bats form harem groups consisting of a single male and numerous females.

LIGHT IN FLIGHT

Gestation takes between ten and twenty weeks depending on the species, after which the female gives birth to a single young. Larger litters are rare, probably because females pregnant with multiple offspring would have difficulty flying. In many species, such as the big-eared bats, pregnant and nursing females separate from the males to form maternity roosts. In caves such roosts can contain thousands of adult females and their young.

Young bats are born blind and scantily haired but generally develop quickly and are left in the roost at night when the females go out to hunt. Within three weeks some are sufficiently well developed to fly. As weaning approaches, the female may encourage them to sample the adult diet, and false vampires offer morsels of chewed flesh to their young to eat.

INSEPARABLE

Vampire bats, belying their fearsome image, have some of the most prolonged periods of postnatal care. The infant bat clings to its mother's teat continuously for up to thirty days, even when she goes out to seek blood. Eventually the growing bat becomes inconveniently heavy and is left at the roost, where it may be suckled by other females that happen to be present.

If the roost is disturbed, a mother may continue carrying her offspring for a few weeks more, by which time it could reach half her body weight. Weaning from a diet of milk to one of fresh blood may not take place until a juvenile common vampire is nine to ten months old.

REACHING MATURITY

Bats usually reach maturity within their first year—though, as in the case of bulldog bats, it may be several years before their maximum weight is attained. Compared with most small mammals, bats

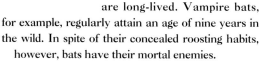

are long-lived. Vampire bats, for example, regularly attain an age of nine years in the wild. In spite of their concealed roosting habits, however, bats have their mortal enemies.

In South America, bats roosting in trees are often caught by snakes like the rainbow boa and large lizards such as black iguanas, and on rare occasions by foraging mammals such as opossums. Even cave-roosting bats may be caught by owls and snakes as they emerge from the entrance; in the open air they are prey both to carnivorous bats and, at dusk, to their most dangerous enemy: the bat falcon, an agile bird of prey. ∎

DANGEROUS

predators, such as the emerald tree boa, are always on the lookout for an easy meal. A careless young bat may be its next victim.

GROWING UP

*The life of a young
Parnell's mustached bat*

A SUCKLING BAT

*stays attached to its mother's
teat even when she is flying.
It develops quickly and is
soon too heavy for her.*

MATING

*Male and female
mate face to face
and hanging
upside down.*

Illustrations John Cox/Wildlife Art Agency

FROM BIRTH TO DEATH

VAMPIRE BAT
GESTATION: 80–120 DAYS
LITTER SIZE: 1
BREEDING: NONSEASONAL;
MATING OCCURS AT ANY TIME
OF YEAR
WEIGHT AT BIRTH: 0.25 oz (5–7 G)
EYES OPEN: 1 WEEK
FIRST FLIGHT: 3 WEEKS
WEANING: 9 MONTHS
INDEPENDENCE: AFTER 1 YEAR
SEXUAL MATURITY: 9 MONTHS
LONGEVITY: UP TO 9 YEARS IN
THE WILD; UP TO 19 IN CAPTIVITY

BULLDOG BAT
GESTATION: 16 WEEKS
LITTER SIZE: 1
BREEDING: BETWEEN NOVEMBER AND
DECEMBER IN PANAMA
WEIGHT AT BIRTH: NOT KNOWN
EYES OPEN: 1 WEEK
FIRST FLIGHT: 3 WEEKS
WEANING: 9–10 MONTHS
INDEPENDENCE: AFTER 1 YEAR;
REACHES ADULT SIZE AT 1 YEAR; ATTAINS
FULL BODY WEIGHT AFTER SEVERAL YEARS
SEXUAL MATURITY: AT LEAST 1 YEAR
LONGEVITY: UP TO 10 YEARS

HANGING AROUND

*Gaining weight rapidly, the
young remain together in the
roosting cave while their
mothers search for food.*

YOUNGSTERS

*start to fly when they
are about three weeks
old, following their
mother and learning
by her example.*

Gary F. McCraken

(in) SIGHT

BAT HAREMS

**Greater spear-nosed bats often roost in
large colonies made up of small, stable
groups. Studies in Trinidad have shown
that the bats form either all-male clusters
or groups of around 30 females with their
young accompanied by a single male.**

**The latter are known as harems
because the male has exclusive breeding
rights to the females and keeps other
males away. A harem male can father
over 50 offspring in about three years.**

VICTIMS OF REPUTATION

FOR CENTURIES, BATS HAVE BEEN THE SUBJECT OF OUTRAGEOUS MYTHS AND MISUNDERSTANDINGS. NOW, AS HUMAN POPULATIONS CONTINUE TO EXPAND, BATS FACE MORE THREATS THAN EVER BEFORE

Bats the world over face pressures imposed by a fast-growing human population. Loss of suitable roosting habitat, decline in food supply, disturbance in caves, and environmental pollution: All are making life increasingly difficult for many bat species. However, there are some pressures on bats that have long been a burden on their survival, often borne out of prejudice and ignorance.

There are some wild creatures that pose little or no threat to humans but consistently disturb people by their presence and even provoke irrational fear. Numbered among them are such animals as cockroaches, spiders, mice, and, more often than not, bats. Just why bats should raise

---

BATS SEEM TO COMBINE ALL THE TRAITS THAT PEOPLE FIND DISTURBING IN ANIMALS, THOUGH THEY POSE LITTLE THREAT

---

such deep-seated fears in so many of us is hard to understand, though they do have many of the traits people seem to find distressing in wild animals.

They are small, fast-moving, capable of abrupt changes in direction, and active at night, when humans are at their most guarded. In addition, they have rapidly fluttering wings, a seemingly erratic, unpredictable manner of flight that can bring them disarmingly close, and a strange, often ferocious appearance. Given these traits, and the fact that bats often find suitable hiding places around human dwellings, it seems inevitable that fears were transformed into superstition and myth.

Folklore frequently, though by no means always, casts bats in a negative light. In Europe, these mysterious creatures of the night have long been associated with the devil and with demons, and

have been depicted in images of hell. The 19th-century French illustrator Gustave Doré showed a legion of batlike souls accompanying the grim reaper in his famous engraving *Triumph of Death*.

FABLED GIANTS

The native peoples of the New World had many legends regarding bats. People of one Arawak settlement in Guyana told of an immense bat that once lived in a secret roost in the mountains. After sunset it would swoop down on the village to seize and devour anyone who strayed out of doors. The desperate villagers only managed to kill it after an old woman sacrificed herself one night: As the bat carried her off, she held out a smoldering stick, the

The grotesque features of some bats (right) *create anxiety and fear among many people, yet only vampires* (above) *actually feed on human blood.*

Doré's Triumph of Death *portrays a host of menacing batlike devils accompanying the grim reaper.*

glow from which revealed the bat's lair.

The vampire bat has given rise to more myths than any other and has heightened human revulsion of bats. When European explorers reached the Americas, they soon heard tales of the vampire bat's habits, sometimes exaggerated. They also saw for themselves that the continent indeed had bats that lived by drinking fresh blood. These stories reached Europe and preyed on existing superstitions. Soon there were fanciful reports that Europe, too, had its blood-eating bats.

FEAR AND LOATHING

A combination of innate fear, myth, and ignorance has made bats widely unpopular, and once there is prejudice against a wild animal, it can be readily and unreasonably accused of all manner of crimes.

Bats have been said to fly deliberately into people's hair, to transfer lice, to steal food, and generally to bring bad luck. Because of such stigma and unpopularity, it is not surprising that these animals have suffered centuries of persecution. Many roost sites have been destroyed, and bats have been poisoned or beaten to death.

Today, those same factors still predispose people to prejudice against bats. When, early in the 20th century, it was discovered that vampire bats can transmit the rabies virus along with several livestock diseases, there was a powerful reaction against bats in the New World. Many thousands of caves used by various species of bat were dynamited, and other bat roosting sites were routinely poisoned and burned, whether or not

---

DESPITE PROBLEMS PRESENTED BY RABIES OUTBREAKS, PREVENTIVE ACTION OFTEN INVOLVES THE BLANKET PERSECUTION OF SEVERAL SPECIES

---

rabies outbreaks had been reported in the area.

Moreover, roost destruction has often taken place regardless of whether the inhabitants are vampire bats or not. Vampires tend to roost in scattered colonies of 100 or fewer bats, in various types of site. But misguided elimination efforts have often been directed at large caves, killing many thousands of other bats.

MISTAKEN IDENTITY

Attempts to identify the target species are often highly flawed. During a recent rabies outbreak in Central America, press publicity suggested that vampire bats could be identified by their lack of a nose leaf—a trait shared by many other species—but one illustration used was, in fact, a photograph of an Asian flying fox. False information such as this has also led people to use poison baits on fruit—food that

in SIGHT

RABIES SCARE

Bats are among the many mammals that can be infected with rabies, a disease that, when untreated, inevitably leads to death. Bites from infected animals provide one way by which the disease is transmitted to livestock and occasionally to people. Because of their widespread distribution, mobility, and blood-feeding habits, vampires are a common carrier of the disease in the Americas.

Though most vampire populations are free from rabies, the drama of a rabies outbreak and the concentrated economic losses that may occur usually result in determined but often misguided efforts to eliminate local vampire populations.

VAMPIRE CONTROL: THE PROBLEM WITH PESTICIDES

Vampires in Central and South America

Over the years, toxic chemicals have been applied in various ways to eradicate or control regional vampire bat populations in order to counter the threat from rabies. These vary from the indiscriminate gassing of roosts, which can kill a wide range of wildlife and contaminate the local environment, to the use of poison baits treated with strychnine intended for individual target species. Poison baits, however, are often ingested by other animals, and the toxins may be passed on to predators and scavengers.

TARGETING THE ENEMY

Modern control methods focus on the behavior of the target animal. Techniques developed in the 1970s use slow-acting anticoagulant pesticides.

When swallowed, these chemicals prevent blood clotting and eventually cause death through internal hemorrhaging. In one control method, vampire bats are captured in mist nets as they home in on corralled cattle at night. The captured animals are smeared with an anticoagulant and released.

When a single treated bat returns to its

CONSERVATION MEASURES

● Education and strict control of antivampire campaigns are the keys to solving the problem of the vampire's continuing conflict with the farmers of Latin America.

● A number of Latin American countries have experimented with a method of control that immunizes the bats themselves against rabies. The control technique makes use of

Background Starfoto/ZEFA

ENDANGERED BY POLLUTION

roost, as many as 40 of its cohabitants may end up swallowing a fatal dose of poison while grooming one another's fur.

The second method involves injecting anticoagulants into the cattle themselves, in concentrations that do not harm the livestock but are fatal to vampire bats feeding on their blood.

PASSING ON THE POISON

However, there is a real possibility that cattle treated repeatedly with such toxins might accumulate dangerous levels of the chemical in their flesh, which could conceivably be passed on to human consumers of their beef. It is important, therefore, that other methods posing a minimal threat to humans be found.

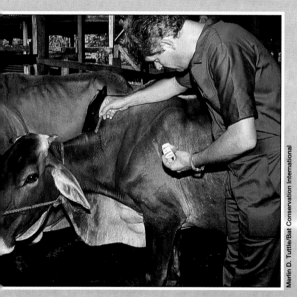

CROP SPRAYING *(BACKGROUND)* IS AN INDISCRIMINATE FORM OF PEST CONTROL; FARMERS NOW TEND TO FOCUS THEIR EFFORTS ON VAMPIRES *(ABOVE)*.

mutual grooming, too, substituting vaccine for anticoagulant. Unfortunately, such plans require expert technicians and large sums of money, both in short supply in Latin America.

● The Texas-based organization Bat Conservation International advises governments on sound environmental policies and also publishes educational material in Spanish.

BATS IN DANGER

THE CHART BELOW SHOWS HOW THE INTERNATIONAL UNION FOR THE CONSERVATION OF NATURE (IUCN) CLASSIFIES THE STATUS OF A NUMBER OF THREATENED BAT SPECIES. THE YEAR IN BRACKETS IS THE DATE OF CLASSIFICATION:

CUBAN FLOWER BAT	INSUFFICIENTLY KNOWN (1990)
JAMAICAN FLOWER BAT	INSUFFICIENTLY KNOWN (1990)
LITTLE LONG-NOSED BAT	VULNERABLE (1990)
MEXICAN LONG-NOSED BAT	VULNERABLE (1990)
NEW ZEALAND SHORT-TAILED BAT	VULNERABLE (1990)
PUERTO RICAN FLOWER BAT	EXTINCT? (1990)

VULNERABLE INDICATES THAT THE ANIMAL WILL MOVE INTO THE ENDANGERED CATEGORY IF THINGS CONTINUE AS THEY ARE. *EXTINCT?* MEANS THE ANIMAL HAS NOT BEEN LOCATED IN THE WILD FOR 50 YEARS AND IS VIRTUALLY CERTAIN TO HAVE BECOME EXTINCT RECENTLY. *INSUFFICIENTLY KNOWN* MEANS IT IS SUSPECTED BUT NOT DEFINITELY KNOWN TO BELONG TO ONE OF THE THREATENED ANIMAL CATEGORIES.

vampire bats never touch but many other New World bats relish.

Rabies is a terribly destructive disease, and the total economic losses from livestock maladies attributed to vampire bites are estimated at about $50 million per year. But the economic benefits of other bats indiscriminately killed during antivampire campaigns is also huge.

SEED DISPERSAL

Bats are important pollinators or seed dispersers for a wide range of valued crop plants that yield products such as avocados, guavas, cashew nuts, cloves, and palm hearts, as well as timber and balsa and raw materials for wines and spirits. They are important seed dispersers for forest plants, and many of the woody plants that colonize clearings in Latin America rely on them, making them indispensable for forest regeneration.

Bats also prey on huge numbers of insects, including mosquitoes, which transmit malaria and

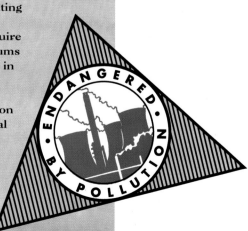

181

ALONGSIDE MAN

THE REAL DRACULA

Centuries before Columbus, Slavic folklore featured supernatural beings known as vampires, believed to be souls of the dead who sucked the blood of sleeping people. This image became fused with a tale concerning Vlad the Impaler, a real-life 15th-century Romanian prince reputed to have held bloodthirsty rule over his domain. Then, in the 16th century, Spanish explorers returned from the New World with tales of blood-feeding bats. In 1897 all these elements were combined in the novelist Bram Stoker's book *Dracula*.

Christopher Lee bares his teeth as Count Dracula in the classic horror film.

Ronald Grant Archive

yellow fever. Since one big cave colony of bats can dominate hundreds of miles of surrounding land, its wanton destruction could have a large-scale detrimental ecological effect.

Indiscriminate persecution is one of many threats that affect phyllostomatoid bats. Other problems can arise from actions not directed at bats themselves but similarly devastating in their impact. As has been noted, migratory populations of Mexican long-nosed bats move north each summer from Mexico into Arizona, feeding from plants such as agave and saguaro cactus.

In recent decades the numbers of these bats reaching the United States has plummeted to just a

Bitter harvest: the agave plant, a staple food for many bat species, is now heavily cropped for use in the tequila industry.

Van der Hilst/Frank Spooner Pictures/Gamma

few thousand. Changes to the bat's habitat may be responsible, including the harvesting of sap from agave plants; the sap is used to make the drinks pulque and tequila. Small-scale tequila production has been a growing source of livelihood in northern Mexico, but the agaves are generally destroyed by harvesting and are seldom replanted

A PROGRAM TO EDUCATE THE PUBLIC ABOUT BATS HAS BEEN ESTABLISHED IN THE UNITED STATES; IT IS HOPED THIS WILL BENEFIT BOTH FARMERS AND BATS

in this region. This has greatly reduced the availability of feeding flowers for bats passing through the region. A cycle of decline may have been started, because the scarcity of bats moving north has hampered pollination of cacti and agaves (and hence reduced plant reproduction) over a still wider area.

CHANGING ATTITUDES

In recent years conservationists and environmental organizations, such as the Texas-based Bat Conservation International (BCI), have brought the plight of many Central and South American bats to the public's attention.

While offering help to those farmers genuinely threatened by bats, they have also begun a program of education intended to differentiate between those bats, such as the vampire, that may be pests and the majority of bats, which cause no harm and may, in fact, be of substantial benefit to the farmers of the region. ■

INTO THE FUTURE

For the phyllostomatoid bats as a whole the future is likely to be one of steady decline in populations as human influence on their environment increases. Throughout Latin America, rapidly rising populations and efforts to expand economic output are causing widespread loss of natural habitats. Wild landscapes are being lost to forestry, mining, road-building, settlement growth, and, above all, the agricultural expansion needed to feed the ever-growing population.

Changes made to the environment will not affect all bats to the same degree, however. Though clearance of tropical forest for ranching, for example, causes great reduction in species diversity, and effectively eliminates forest-dependent species such as fruit-eating bats, it can provide good hunting habitat for some insect-eating species that catch

PREDICTION

BANS ON BANDING

Bat studies involving banding or tagging, already the subject of a moratorium in the United States, look likely to be banned in Latin America. Many bats were distressed or injured by incompetent researchers in projects of often dubious scientific value.

prey on the wing. Likewise, the spread of livestock farming has proven of enormous benefit to vampire bats, whose populations are now unnaturally large, much to the irritation of the farmers.

For the vast majority of bats, though, the future promises a gradual reduction in numbers. Many species face particular problems. The Jamaican fig-eating bat is being squeezed by intensive agricultural development on its island; at a series of gold mines in the southern United States where cyanide is used in the extraction process, bats are common victims of accidental poisoning.

A SECURE FUTURE?

Among those most threatened are two scarce plant-pollinating species, the lesser long-nosed and hog-nosed bats. Millions of others will continue to be killed indiscriminately by the destruction of their roosts during antivampire fever. Even if the bats escape, the disturbance may prevent them returning to roost, and other suitable sites may not be available. Ironically, unless efforts are made to educate people about bats, only the dreaded vampire will be able to look forward to a secure future. ∎

THREATENED ISLANDERS

The *1990 IUCN Red List of Threatened Animals* lists six phyllostomatoid bats as being in imminent danger. Two, the Mexican long-nosed and the lesser long-nosed bat, have declined because of widespread changes to their dryland habitats. The others, however, are island species.

Island wildlife is highly vulnerable to encroachment on its habitat, persecution, and interference from introduced animals. Wild populations of island species are relatively small, space is limited, and many have evolved in isolation, leaving them with poor defenses against mainland predators and competitors. The Puerto Rican flower bat, for one, is now almost certainly extinct.

Illustration Peter David Scott/Wildlife Art Agency

THE ROLE OF BCI

Conservation efforts to help bats in Latin America have so far made little progress; it will be several years at least before education campaigns and protection measures begin to take effect. However, one organization, Bat Conservation International (BCI), is dedicated to getting things moving.

Based in the United States—in Austin, Texas—but with members from over fifty countries, it is concerned with the status of bats worldwide. Its successes since its founding in 1982 have included the purchase of key bat sites, support for conservation programs and research, and the preparation of educational material in both English and Spanish.

BCI has actively campaigned for improvements in protective legislation, including the placing of threatened bats on the CITES list of wild species banned from international trade, and recently it joined up with Texas A & M University to create an academic unit with the aim of training biologists specializing in bat conservation.

SMALL BATS

RELATIONS

Small bats belong to the order Chiroptera. All bats are members of the order and include:

SAMOAN FLYING FOX

HAMMERHEAD BAT

DAWN BATS

THUMBLESS BATS

VAMPIRE BATS

Merlin D. Tuttle/Oxford Scientific Films

CLASSIFICATION

Bats make up more than a quarter of all known mammal species. There are two suborders: the insect-eating bats, Microchiroptera, known for their sonar hunting and navigation technique, and the larger flying foxes, Megachiroptera, which eat fruit and rely on their eyesight. The 12 families in this article are from 3 of the 4 Microchiroptera superfamilies.

ORDER

Chiroptera
(bats)

SUBORDER

Microchiroptera
(insect-eating bats)

SUPERFAMILY

Emballonuroidea
(sheath-tailed bats and allies)

SUPERFAMILY

Rhinolophoidea
(horseshoe bats and allies)

SUPERFAMILY

Vespertilionoidea
(free-tailed bats and allies)

WINGED GARGOYLES

IF PRESSED, MOST OF US WOULD ADMIT THAT WE FIND BATS HORRIBLY UGLY. BUT WHY ARE THEIR FACES SO CONTORTED? THE ANSWERS MAY HELP TO UNRAVEL SOME OF NATURE'S MOST SOPHISTICATED MYSTERIES

A medieval villager enters a churchyard to offer up prayers on All Souls' Day. He pushes open a tomb's doorway and startles a roosting colony of horseshoe bats, which flit around him chaotically. Frantically running for the nearest church or tavern, the peasant would have had little time to reflect on the marvels of a mammal capable of real flight.

Bat anatomy reflects adaptations that strengthen its aerodynamic qualities. The key modifications are in the long, fine bones of the forearm and fingers. Between them stretches the patagium—the wing membrane. A bat's center of gravity is well to the front in the chest, which itself is large enough to hold a powerful beating heart. The smooth pelt makes the body more streamlined.

Bats form the order Chiroptera (ky-RAHP-te-ruh), or "hand-wings." The ability to use echolocation—a sophisticated natural "sonar" for navigating and detecting prey—distinguishes the members of the

185

SIGHT

THE BUMBLEBEE BAT

The smallest mammal in the world is Kitti's hog-nosed bat, which has only ever been observed at two caves in southwest Thailand, near the infamous River Kwai. This tiny bat is sometimes called the bumblebee bat because of its size. It has a wingspan of about 6 in (150 mm) but a head-and-body length of only 1.14–1.29 in (29–33 mm) and it weighs no more than 0.07 ounces (2 g).

The discovery of this minuscule species by Kitti Thonglongya in 1973 both excited and perplexed mammalogists seeking to classify it. Eventually they decided that it should remain a single-species genus within its own family, Craseonycteridae, or hog-nosed bats.

suborder Microchiroptera (my-cro-ky-RAHP-te-ruh), which comprises 18 families arranged in four superfamilies. This section looks at the horseshoe bats, Rhinolophoidea (REE-no-lo-FOID-ee-yuh), the sheath-tailed bats, Emballonuroidea (em-BAL-on-yu-ROID-ee-yuh), and the free-tailed bats, Vespertilionoidea (VES-per-ti-lee-on-OID-ee-yuh).

EVOLUTIONARY ADVANTAGES

Most species within the suborder Microchiroptera are insect-eaters, and fossil evidence suggests that they all were once. The fact that most bats remained insect-eaters is equally important. By not diversifying their food sources, and thereby evolving tooth and jaw adaptations for eating plants and other foods, bats had to refine their skills as insect-hunters or lose out to competition. Bats developed from tree-dwelling insectivorous mammals, which gradually evolved membranes that enabled them to take short gliding flights. Remarkably well-preserved fossils found in Germany indicate that bats had evolved the powers of sustained flight and echolocation as early as 50 million years ago—zoologists recognized the long bones of the forearms and fingers, and the stomach contents of the fossilized bats contained the wing scales of nocturnal moths.

So, bats found themselves with two distinct evolutionary advantages early on: the ability to fly and the capacity to hunt and navigate when their competitors were "grounded." How, then, did they prevent other bats from jamming their signals? The answer

The "horseshoe" around the nostrils of a greater horseshoe bat aids its echolocation capabilities.

Stephen Dalton/Oxford Scientific Films

186

The Persian trident bat (below) *is named after the three-pronged leaf above its nostrils.*

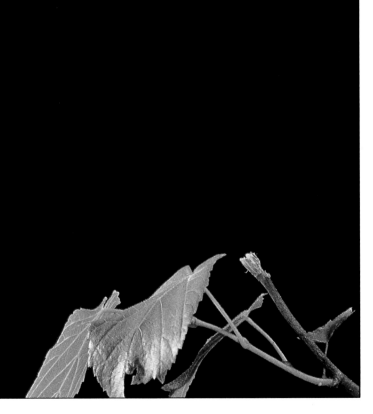

gives a clue about the profusion of bat species as well as their appearance, which is often described as "grotesque."

Most bat adaptations are concentrated on the head. Silhouetted against the fading light of a dusk sky, many bat species are indistinguishable; but seen at rest, bats reveal their real diversity. The variation of facial features lies behind much of the suborder's classification and leads to such common names as hog-nosed, slit-faced, leaf-nosed, and funnel-eared.

Horseshoe bats take their name from the distinctively shaped fleshy structure surrounding the nose. This nose leaf acts as a megaphone for the ultrasonic signals emitted from the nostrils. Their ears are also specially adapted: They can swivel back and forth, even independently of each other, as the bat seeks to receive the sonar echoes.

The Old World leaf-nosed bat · family, Hipposideridae (hip-o-sid-ER-id-eye), has more than forty species. These have sometimes been classified as a subfamily of the horseshoe bats because of the similarly shaped nose leaf. However, the area above the nostrils is highly modified into a range of forks, prongs, and other structures. Like horseshoe bats, they fly with their mouths closed, emitting far-reaching, beamed pulses through their nostrils.

Not all of the many bat variations are confined to the head, however. The four species of the mouse-tailed bat family, mostly natives of the Middle East, have long, naked tails that match the head-and-body length. These bats are also noted for their ability to build up an abdominal layer of fat that equals the bat's original body weight. The bats can survive off this fat for several weeks during colder weather when there is a shortage of insect food. Mouse-tailed bats will often spend this period of torpor in ruined buildings or temples. Some species are believed to have colonized pyramids for more than 3,000 years.

The disc-winged bats of the family Thyropteridae (thigh-rop-TER-id-eye) get their name from the disc-shaped suction pads on the base of each thumb and on the ankles. These bats live in Central and South America. These suction discs, connected to the bat by short stalks, enable it to climb up smooth tree trunks or leaves. They also allow these bats to roost right side up.

FALSE VAMPIRES AND GHOSTS

The Australian false vampire bat, like the other four false vampire species, swoops silently down onto a smaller bat or rodent and stops to chew it briefly before eating the flesh. The first European settlers in Australia mistook this action as sucking the blood of the prey. The bat's popular name of ghost bat (because of its pale coloration) is probably suggested by this unearned reputation for vampirism.

The white bat of Central America is also known as the ghost bat, although this name is unavoidable given the bat's bright white coloration. No other bat, apart from rare albinos, can match this coloration. Strangely, the white coloring does not seem to make this bat more conspicuous to predators. ∎

THE "OTHER" BATS

There are a number of important differences between insectivorous bats, which make up the majority of bat species, and the Old World fruit bats, or megachiropterans. Fruit bats are considerably larger, with wingspans of up to 5 ft (1.5 m), and a reddish brown coat that has led them to be nicknamed flying foxes. Fruit bats have much larger eyes and use sight, rather than echolocation, for navigation and hunting.

Roosting in trees rather than in caves, they set off on nightly feeding trips of up to 42 miles (70 km). Their size, as well as the steady beat of their wings, immediately distinguishes them from any variety of insect-eating bat.

Color illustrations Simon Turvey/Wildlife Art Agency

THE INSECT-EATING BATS' FAMILY TREE

Insect-eating bats, or microchiropterans, are grouped into four superfamilies, with classification largely based on physical structure. With new species constantly being discovered, and even known species being poorly studied, classification is somewhat fluid and subject to some dispute.

SHEATH-TAILED BATS AND ALLIES
Emballonuroidea
(em-BAL-on-yu-ROID-ee-yuh)

The most numerous family within this superfamily is the Emballonuridae, with some forty species. The "sheath" is a distinctive membrane that stretches between the hind legs. The other families are Rhinopomatidae, or mouse-tailed bats, and Craseonycteridae with its single species, Kitti's hog-nosed bat—which is the smallest bat species in the world.

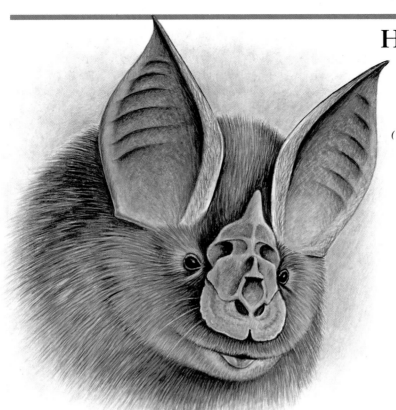

HORSESHOE BATS AND ALLIES

Rhinolophoidea
(*REE-no-lo-FOID-ee-yuh*)

A horseshoe-shaped structure on the face distinguishes most of the 51 members of the Rhinolophidae family. This shape is modified in the 40 species of the Hipposideridae family of leaf-nosed bats. The other families are the Nycteridae, or slit-faced bats, and the Megadermatidae, or false vampire bats.

FREE-TAILED BATS AND ALLIES

Vespertilionoidea
(*VES-per-tih-lee-on-OID-ee-yuh*)

Members of the free-tailed bat family, Molossidae, have long, rodentlike tails and narrow wings. The 80 species are native to warm regions. The other families have narrower ranges: Myzopodidae comprises one species of sucker-footed bat in Madagascar. The funnel-eared bats, Natalidae, smoky bats, Furipteridae, and disc-winged bats, Thyropteridae, are all native to the American tropics. The vesper, or common bat family Vespertilionidae (covered in an earlier entry), is the most widespread.

MICROCHIROPTERA
(INSECT-EATING BATS)

ANATOMY:
THE GREATER HORSESHOE BAT

THE WINGS

are used to scoop up the bat's insect prey rather than catching it directly with the mouth. The bat can manipulate the membrane like a hand to put food in the mouth.

THE EARS

are typically large. While in flight the bat can move its ears backward and forward as quickly as 60 times a second as it patrols the airwaves for sound signals.

THE EYES

are small, and the field of vision is reduced by the large nose leaf, indicating that sight is less important than sound.

THE "HORSESHOE"

is the fleshy middle section around the nose. Above the nose is the erect lancet, and between these two features is the sella. These features combine to act as a sonar megaphone, which can be adjusted to direct sound wherever the bat chooses.

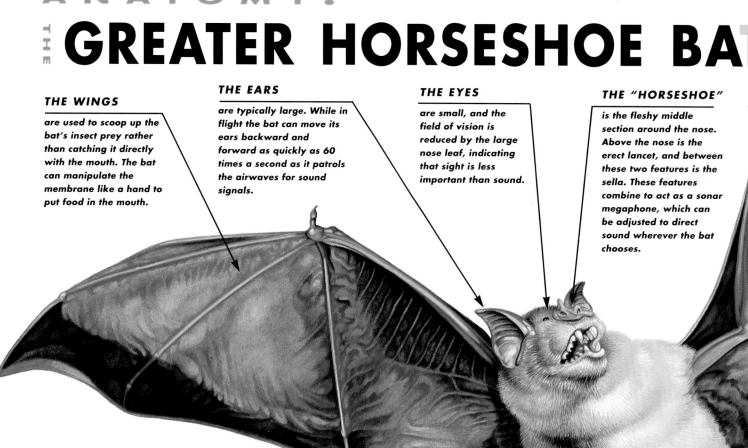

The greater horseshoe bat (above) is one of the largest members of the Rhinolophid family. The lesser horseshoe, one of the smallest members, is only about two-thirds as long, or about the size of a house mouse.

X RAY

GREATER HORSESHOE BAT SKELETON

Light, slender bones and a comparatively "snub" skull reflect how bats have developed birdlike adaptations for flight. The hind legs are comparatively small to compensate for the enlarged forelegs, which form the wings. Enormously elongated finger bones provide the supporting "struts" to the wings. These are fully articulated and can be folded neatly to wrap the wings around the body when the bat hangs up to rest.

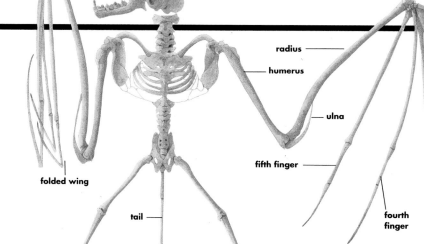

thumb
(first finger

radius

humerus

ulna

second finger

fifth finger

folded wing

tail

fourth finger

third finger

X-ray illustrations Elisabeth Smith

CLASSIFICATION

GENUS: *RHINOLOPHUS*
SPECIES: *FERRUMEQUINUM*

SIZE

HEAD–BODY LENGTH: 4.5–5 IN (11–12.5 CM)
TAIL LENGTH: 1–1.5 IN (2.5–4 CM)
WINGSPAN: 13–14 IN (33–35 CM)
WEIGHT: 0.5–1.2 OZ (13–34 G)
WEIGHT AT BIRTH: 0.07–0.1 OZ (2–3 G)

COLORATION

PALE BROWN COAT WITH REDDISH TINT

FEATURES

LARGE EARS
**MIDDLE RIDGE OF NASAL STRUCTURE IS
CONCAVE WHEN SEEN FROM ABOVE**
**MUSCULAR LANCET ABOVE NOSTRILS AND SELLA
BETWEEN THEM**
**TWO NONFUNCTIONING "DUMMY" TEATS ON
FEMALE'S ABDOMEN**

THE WINGS

are broad with rounded ends. The greater horseshoe is rather slow and fluttering in flight, but swoops down like a hawk on ground-dwelling beetles. Like other horseshoe bats, it wraps its wings around its body when roosting rather than folding them.

EARS AND NOSES

Ear size and shape range widely. Some species have an extra lobe called a tragus; others, such as the horseshoe bats, have extremely mobile ears capable of moving independently. The long ears of false vampire bats are connected by a membrane, whereas most species native to northern Europe have smaller, less mobile ears. Bats recognize sounds of 50,000–200,000 Hz (vibrations a second).

Most bats have elaborate, fleshy structures surrounding their noses. Muscular, and sensitive to the vibrations emitted from the nostrils, these nose leaves can assume grotesque shapes in some species. The nose leaves thereby provide easy means of distinguishing different bat species.

FALSE VAMPIRE BAT

**MOUSE-TAILED BAT
(SUPERFAMILY EMBALLONUROIDEA)**

OLD WORLD LEAF-NOSED BAT

TEETH

Most insect-eaters have sharp-edged molars with a W-shaped pattern of ridges. The upper and lower ridges meet rather like scissor blades to grind the tough shells of insects.

scissor-action teeth

WING MUSCLES

The various sections of the patagium are controlled by finger flexing and by muscles set within the membrane itself. An important muscle from the shoulder to the wrist controls the leading-edge patagium section; contraction of this muscle, for example, adjusts the curve of the wing surface. Limb muscles act to contract the skeleton (right).

shoulder blade

humerus

radius

large brain-case to cope with sound analysis

muscle

wrist (fingers not shown here)

contracted limb

wrist

Main illustration Rachel Lockwood/Wildlife Art Agency

STEALTH FIGHTERS

BATS HAVE AN ALMOST OWL-LIKE ABILITY TO SEEK AND DESTROY BY NIGHT. EQUIPPED TO TARGET THEIR INSECT PREY IN UTTER DARKNESS, THEY HOME IN ON SILENT WINGS TO LAUNCH THEIR ATTACK

Deep inside a limestone cave there is silence, broken only by the rhythmic drip of water onto the cavern floor. The temperature is a constant 54°F (12°C), although subfreezing temperatures have brought several weeks of snow and sleet outside. Stalactites hang like icicles from the vault of the cave. Among them is a knot of reddish brown fur; on closer inspection, this is revealed as a group of about 100 hibernating horseshoe bats.

Horseshoe bats sometimes migrate great distances in order to find the best site for hibernation, which might become the winter home for thousands of individuals. Large caves, with their seclusion, slight dampness, and constant but low temperature, make ideal hibernation sites, but bats will also hibernate in small caves, crevices, or mines. There the body temperature of the bats will fall, and with it the metabolic rate, until the bats reach a state of suspended animation.

There is a good reason why horseshoe bats and many other bat species hibernate through the coldest months of the year: There is no food. The insects are gone from the skies, and with them the chance for bats to maintain their energy-demanding metabolism. The bats respond by spending the winter months in energy-saving inactivity.

Hibernation highlights another factor that singles out bats. Most mammals are warm-blooded, or homiothermal. This means that they are able to maintain their body temperature at a constant level. Such animals regulate their own heat levels, using thermal insulation in colder periods and releasing heat in summer with mechanisms such as sweating and panting. Bats, by contrast, are heterotherms. This means that they allow their body temperature to fluctuate—sometimes greatly—and the ability to let the temperature drop in colder months is essential for their survival.

The body temperature of bats living in temperate climates will dip to 41–45°F (5–7°C) during hibernation. The corresponding reduction in metabolic rate is dramatic. Zoologists have estimated that oxygen consumption of hibernating bats is only about 1 percent of that in their active state. But even with these vastly reduced energy demands, bats still need nourishment to take them through these periods of up to six months. So they begin building fat supplies to see them through the winter. Bats begin storing high-energy fat reserves from late summer onward. As autumn sets in, they even allow their body temperatures to drop during daytime inactivity. This induces a daily torpor, a type of minihibernation that reduces immediate food demands in favor of longer-term fat supplies.

Many of the sheath-tailed bats (above) *have small wing pockets that secrete a musky scent.*

Pat Morris/Ardea

Babs & Bert Wells/Oxford Scientific Films

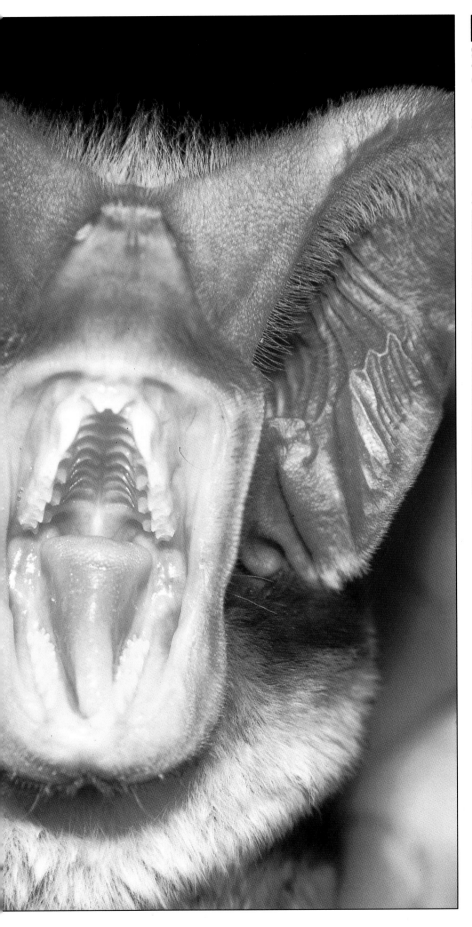

KEY FACTS

● Bats have a greater variety of temperature-regulating mechanisms than any other order of mammals. They can withstand temperatures almost as low as freezing point (32°F/0°C), for example, and their veined wings give them a higher heat-radiating surface than in mammals of similar size.

● Echolocation, primarily a means of navigating and hunting, also helps mothers and their offspring. The young cry out from the moment they are first removed from the teat. Those same cries, together with maternal responses, provide a highly individualized means of communication.

● Awakening from hibernation, a bat builds up heat through two mechanisms, each triggered by the nervous system. The first involves the skeletal muscles, which generate heat through shivering. The second is a fatty neck gland that contains droplets of fat; these can be rapidly oxidized, thereby generating heat with a biochemical reaction.

Just before winter most hibernating species have built up fat reserves equivalent to one-third of their body weight. The fatty deposits are concentrated in the tissue below the skin—around the neck, between the shoulder blades, and on the flanks. Sometimes only a few milligrams (a fraction of an ounce) of this fat is left at the end of winter; this small amount is used in the final waking from the hibernating state.

Temporary changes in weather, bringing cold or rain or other factors reducing the insect food supply, can trigger a state of torpor in bats. Even bats that do not hibernate will achieve this state, which is similar to that of the seasonal fat-building phases of hibernating species. Bats also seem to possess an "internal clock" that guides their nocturnal behavior in the warmer months. Most species tend to leave their roosts soon after sunset and return just before sunrise. The cue for this pattern depends on changes in light intensity. As a result, progressively later sunsets in the late spring cue correspondingly later "wake-up calls," and the process is reversed after the summer solstice. ■

The impressive teeth of this giant free-tailed bat are designed to crunch up insects on the wing.

HABITATS

Associating bats with the ghoulish and macabre is unfair, but nevertheless understandable. Medieval Europeans could not have known about vampire bats, the only species that could ever really have been considered a danger to humans; yet if a computer were fed data on what factors constitute an ideal bat roosting site—darkness, quiet, constant temperature, a hint of dampness—it might well conclude that a crypt was the obvious choice. But bats have shown themselves to be adaptable, occurring in nearly every natural habitat except the furthest polar extremes. Insect-eating species proliferate in the tropics because of the plentiful food supply, near-constant climate, and ample natural cover.

Those living in more temperate climates are concentrated in areas that provide shelter and at least a seasonal abundance of insects—enough to build up fatty reserves to nourish them during periods of hibernation or torpor. Winter roosting sites are essential for these temperate species to fulfill the strict demands imposed by hibernation. European horseshoe bats tend to spend the entire year quite close to their winter roosts, but some temperate species will migrate short distances between summer and winter roosts.

> IN THE GEOGRAPHICAL AND ECOLOGICAL RANGE OF THEIR HABITATS, BATS ARE SURPASSED ONLY BY RODENTS AND HUMANS

The winter migrations can be in any direction—not necessarily south—usually toward the nearest cave system. However, none of the bats studied in this section can compare with the migratory patterns of noctules of the family Vespertilionidae, some of which migrate more than 1,400 miles (2,300 km) from central Russia to the Caucasus.

SUITABLE SITES

As nocturnal creatures, bats depend on daytime roosting places that offer concealment from predators and humans. Some rare exceptions can build or modify their own roosting sites, but most insectivores spend the daylight hours in ready-made sites that offer safety and quiet. Natural caves are the obvious choice, but bats can roost successfully in mines, tunnels, tombs, and crevices, if they are sheltered. Several disc-winged bats usually roost in a tube formed by a young, curled banana leaf. They are forced to find a new roosting spot almost daily, as their original leaf unfurls.

Sylvestris/NHPA

Bats appear ungainly on solid ground, crawling with the use of their thumb hooks and feet (above).

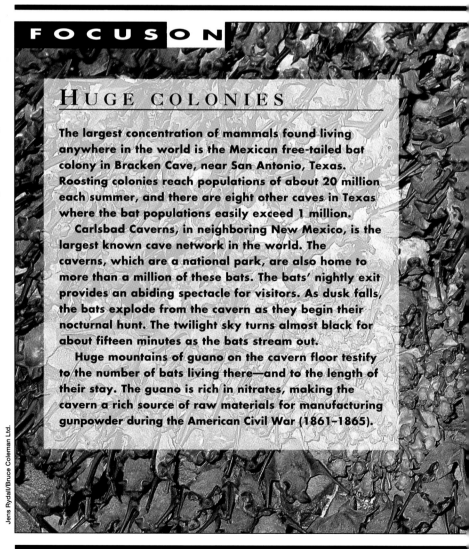

Jens Rydall/Bruce Coleman Ltd.

FOCUS ON

HUGE COLONIES

The largest concentration of mammals found living anywhere in the world is the Mexican free-tailed bat colony in Bracken Cave, near San Antonio, Texas. Roosting colonies reach populations of about 20 million each summer, and there are eight other caves in Texas where the bat populations easily exceed 1 million.

Carlsbad Caverns, in neighboring New Mexico, is the largest known cave network in the world. The caverns, which are a national park, are also home to more than a million of these bats. The bats' nightly exit provides an abiding spectacle for visitors. As dusk falls, the bats explode from the cavern as they begin their nocturnal hunt. The twilight sky turns almost black for about fifteen minutes as the bats stream out.

Huge mountains of guano on the cavern floor testify to the number of bats living there—and to the length of their stay. The guano is rich in nitrates, making the cavern a rich source of raw materials for manufacturing gunpowder during the American Civil War (1861–1865).

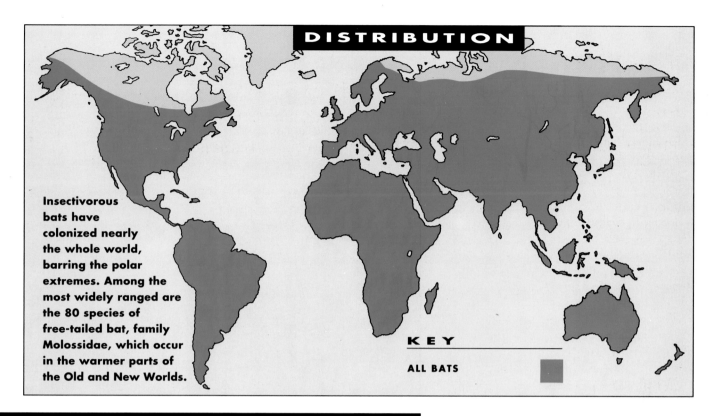

DISTRIBUTION

Insectivorous bats have colonized nearly the whole world, barring the polar extremes. Among the most widely ranged are the 80 species of free-tailed bat, family Molossidae, which occur in the warmer parts of the Old and New Worlds.

KEY

ALL BATS

Choices of daytime roost may be opportunistic, with bats choosing the only available shelter. Some species will roost in between aerial roots of trees or in empty bird nests. Caves, on the other hand, represent the other extreme by hosting huge bat colonies over long periods (*see Focus, left*).

Permanent food supplies account for roosting sites with remarkable longevity, but many bat species switch sites in their continuing search for new food sources. The proboscis bat of Latin America has a range of roosts, but always near water. It patrols waterways, snapping up insects flying close to the water surface. Colonies of these bats move from site to site, roosting on rocks or branches. Sometimes they roost quite openly on cliff faces; their lichen-colored coats act as camouflage.

Bats have adapted to humans throughout much of their range, roosting in houses, churches, and ancient, overgrown temples. The tailless leaf-nosed bat of Southeast Asia has colonized human edifices that have been abandoned much more recently. On Taiwan it roosts not just in its traditional cave sites, but also in pillboxes built by the invading Japanese army in the 1940s.

Slit-faced bats live mainly in the wooded savanna or dry country of Africa. This terrain provides a rich and varied diet for the bats, including frogs, birds, and other bats, but it is short of obvious roosting sites. Slit-faced bats, as a result, shelter alone, in pairs, or at most in small family groups. Roosting sites are also born out of necessity. When caves and dense foliage are not available, slit-faced bats will roost in porcupine or aardvark burrows. ∎

HUNTING

Why do bats hunt at night? One obvious reason is that birds had staked their claim to daytime aerial hunting some 90 million years before the first bats took to the air. During that time birds had a chance to diversify and specialize, allowing them to fit nearly every ecological niche available. A look at the present-day distribution of bats—covering most of every continent except Antarctica—indicates that the Chiroptera order has spread as successfully as have birds. The key to this distribution has been their system of emitting and receiving ultrasound signals known as echolocation.

The echolocation method that insect-eating bats use for navigation and hunting is one of the miracles of nature. Amazingly, it can even operate in the close confines of a cave inhabited by millions of bats. Consider, for example, the multimillion hordes of Mexican free-tailed bats in the caves of Texas and New Mexico. The exodus at dusk, when the potential for a sonar "jam" would seem likeliest, actually passes off without mishap. To appreciate this navigational marvel, imagine a squadron of supersonic jet fighters flying through the Channel Tunnel and meeting another coming in the opposite direction. Then multiply the number of aircraft by about a hundred. We can even put the echolocation technique to the test by tossing a pebble or twig in the air near a bat. The inquisitive bat will follow it through its brief trajectory, spiraling around it as it falls to the ground.

HOW DOES IT WORK?

There are two main methods used by bats. In the more basic system, the bat emits sound pulses and listens to their echo as they bounce off an object. If the echo returns slowly, the object is distant, whereas if it returns rapidly, the object is close by. And by the quality of the echo, the bat can distinguish the type and scale of the object. So a small, moving object in the night sky will tempt the bat to take a closer look.

Another location method uses an effect that we term Doppler. The bat sends out a stream of pulses, all the while analyzing the echo. While it moves toward a moth, it actually catches up on the echoes, so that they arrive more frequently and their tone, or "note," rises in pitch. Likewise, if the moth flies away, the tone drops. You can hear the same effect when an ambulance or fire engine passes you in the street: As it passes you, the siren appears to drop in pitch.

Having tuned in to its prey, the bat moves in for the kill. While previously scanning the skies, it will have been sending out 5–20 pulses per second. But in the final instants as it closes in on a moth, the pulses rise into a high-pitched scream, which gives the bat a precise "sound-picture" of its victim.

Bats are not unique in their ability to make use of ultrasound detection; the skill is common in shrews and other primitive insectivores. Bats

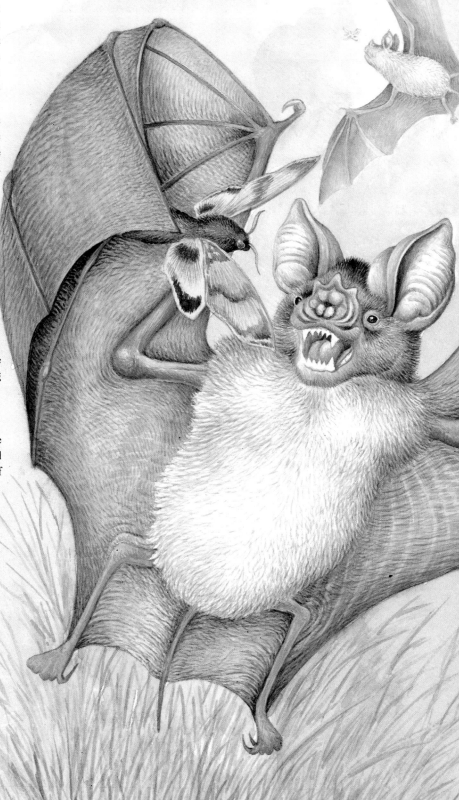

(in) SIGHT

FLY CATCHING

The African yellow-winged bat is a member of the family Megadermatidae, or false vampire bats. Unlike other members of the family, however, the yellow-winged bat feeds exclusively on insects. It usually roosts in acacia trees, which attract huge numbers of swarming insects when they are in bloom.

The bat has evolved a method of nocturnal hunting that is unusual among bats. Like a flycatcher, it perches on (or rather, under) a branch, scanning its immediate area for prey. When it spots an insect, the bat swoops down to snap it up. Then it returns to a perch to eat the catch.

Illustration Robin Budden/Wildlife Art Agency

Peter Ward/Oxford Scientific Films

SOUND ANALYSIS

Leaf-nosed bats (above) *have finely detailed nose leaves, which are thought to focus echoes. They may also shield the bat's ears from emitted pulses so that its hearing is preserved for assessing the echoes.*

refined it initially as a navigational necessity for nocturnal flying, but as the main reason for flying was to gain the high ground in insect hunting, this navigational system underwent a parallel evolution as a hunting aid.

The first bats were—and most bat species remain today—insectivores. Nocturnal flight requires a great deal of energy to support the bat's high metabolic rate, and scientists have estimated that bats need to consume at least one-quarter of their own body weight each night. That translates into a huge amount of insects, which accounts for the need to hunt effectively. Being able to locate nocturnal obstacles and to follow the erratic course of insects solves only part of a bat's hunting problem; it also needs to be able to maneuver quickly in midair. It is worth remembering that a bat wing is

simply a membrane stretched across its elongated fingers, articulated by several minuscule, fine muscles. With deft movements of its outer fingers—and therefore the outer edges of its wings—a bat can change direction or stop almost instantaneously.

These lightning-quick turns are the hallmark of most insect-eating bats. Like acrobatic aircraft they bank and roll, even "stall"—rapidly rotating their wings to hover—and then turn to fly straight up or down. Greater horseshoe bats, fairly slow flyers within the suborder, are still able to dart in and out of undergrowth as they pursue prey at altitudes of 20 ft (6 m) or lower.

The large Malay leaf-nosed bat is another slow flyer but has adapted its diet to suit its habitat. Hundreds of these bats emerge from caves or buildings at dusk and begin to forage around flowers. There they will snap up any insects they find, sometimes tearing open figs to dig out insect larvae while at the same time eating the fig pulp and seed. Tomb bats, found from Madagascar to Southeast Asia, are more skilled at insect hunting high up in the sky. At dusk they climb as high as 330 ft (100 m) in search of insect prey. They hunt at progressively lower altitudes as night wears on.

The velvety free-tailed bat of Central America alternates hunting expeditions with constant returns to its roost. It is a good hunter, cramming as many insects as possible into its large cheek pouches before returning to the roost to consume them. It has been suggested that this behavior evolved as a way of minimizing the time that the bats are exposed to predators.

The above examples, although widely varied, use echolocation in a similar way. When a bat is flying in open spaces, it emits only one or two signals per wing-flapping cycle. It increases its transmission once an echo is received and issues more and more signals as it nears the object. Just before reaching the object, it sends out a long series of very short signals in order to get a precise "fix" on its target.

Echolocation has proved to be an immensely successful method of hunting, but it does create special problems of its own. With a mouth full of freshly caught prey, a bat can be temporarily "blinded" as it is unable to emit its characteristic sonar squeaks. To counter this problem, many bat

---

BATS CAN USE MULTIPLE-TONE SOUNDS, OR "HARMONIES," TO ANALYZE COMPLEX SURROUNDINGS SUCH AS FORESTS

---

species have developed means of squeaking through their noses or through elaborate nasal outgrowths. These adaptations are the defining feature of whole groups of bats, such as the leaf-nosed, hog-nosed, and horseshoe bats.

While bats have specialized in their methods of navigating and hunting, insects have responded with some defensive adaptations of their own. Some New World moths are able to tune in to the frequency of bat sonar; they drop to the ground if they detect an approaching bat. Other insects can jam the bat's signal or emit high-frequency sounds designed to convince the bat that the insect is inedible. Other insect defenses are more conventional, such as going into a type of tailspin that bats find difficult to follow.

AMAZING FACTS

● **Two species of bird also use echolocation for navigation: the oilbird of tropical South America and the cave swiftlet of southern India and Southeast Asia. Their "sonar" systems are more basic than that of the bats. The oilbird, for example, can only distinguish objects with a diameter of 14 in (35 cm) or greater—the size of another oilbird.**

● **Dolphins, which use echolocation to hunt fish, become entangled in discarded fishing nets because, like oilbirds, their sonar is ineffective on tiny objects—such as the fine lines of a mesh.**

● **Bats emit sounds in the range of 20–120 kHz (20,000 to 120,000 Hertz, or wavelengths per second). Only occasionally do bats dip into the range audible to humans (up to 20 kHz); the bat sounds are heard as short clicks.**

● **Zoologists estimate that a single colony of Mexican free-tailed bats may consume more than 6,000 tons of insects each summer.**

Illustration Philip Hood/Wildlife Art Agency

BIG EARS

The Australian false vampire does not need to use echolocation; its huge, highly sensitive ears help it to detect ground-based prey.

Some bats hunt on the ground. Even here, highly sensitive ears can be an advantage, especially when coupled with echolocation. The largest Old World insectivorous species is the Australian false vampire bat; it is also one of the few bat species that hunt by ambushing its prey on the ground. Its ears are large and sensitive, and the bat listens for the sounds of its prey directly, without using sonar.

In this way the false vampire bat can remain in a tree until a sound catches its interest; it might come from a small mammal, a bird, or even a large insect. The bat turns its ears in the direction of the sound and begins to trace its progress. It waits for the animal to come closer, perhaps within three feet (a meter) or so before switching to echolocation. Having found its prey by listening directly and then tracing it with echolocation, the false vampire takes off. It flies around the immediate area, fixing the exact coordinates, and then hovers some 8–12 in (20–30 cm) above its prey. Only then will it swoop down for the kill. The bat covers the prey with its wings and lands on it; a bite to the neck delivers the coup de grâce.

Since much of this hunting technique relies on listening, false vampire bats have become adept at recognizing the sounds of their favorite prey. These bats have been observed at rest and then suddenly alerted by a sound inaudible to the human observer. In fact, the bat has probably just detected the ultrasonic cry of an abandoned baby mouse.

The ten species of slit-faced bat are native to Africa and as far north as Corfu. They are noted for hunting ground-based prey such as large insects, spiders, frogs, and fish. Most species flutter around trees and bushes, waiting for prey, but they will even enter houses in search of insects. ■

Among those species that hunt insects on the wing (below), *most patrol a regular "beat" each night.*

Stephen Dalton/Oxford Scientific Films

ROOSTING

A bat's night of hunting ends as the first light of dawn begins to brighten the sky. That sets off the "alarm" in the bat's internal clock, signaling the time to return to its daytime roost. There the bat spends the hours until dusk, sheltering in a cave, a tree, a crevice, or even a burrow or nest abandoned by other animals. Some species, such as horseshoe bats, will even roost in unused lofts in forts, castles, and churches. Bats might roost singly, in pairs, or in colonies numbered in millions, but the requirements for a roost are similar: stable temperature and moisture, concealment from predators, and protection from the elements.

Some bat species select a roost site where the temperature is equal to their resting body temperature; in such a place they need make no adjustment to sleep comfortably. Other species may deliberately choose a roosting environment that is slightly cooler, so that their bodies relax into a mild torpor and economize on energy.

Caves support the largest populations of roosting insectivorous bats; they are also the preferred roosting site if a choice is available. Bats roost in niches and recesses in the cave roof, or from projections and cracks in the walls of the cave. A single cave

Jens Rydell/Bruce Coleman Ltd.

(in)SIGHT

WHY HIBERNATE?

If birds native to temperate climates are prepared to travel across continents twice a year in migration, then why do most bats stay put and hibernate? One simple response is to turn the question on its head: Why do most birds not hibernate? It would save them energy loss, exposure to predators, and poor weather.

The key to the answer is the inability of birds to "switch off" and "switch on," metabolically speaking. As temperatures fall and insect prey disappear from the skies, a bat enters a state of such extreme torpidity that its heartbeat is only about 2.5 percent of normal. Birds lack this capacity and so must find prey-rich areas.

But the answer is not always clear-cut. Certain bats do make long migrations and still hibernate. Greater horseshoe bats, for example, travel far to find the right winter quarters—deep in caves and crevices—in which to hibernate in the thousands.

Illustration Evi Antoniou

WARMER CLIMES

The funnel-eared bats have little need for hibernation quarters in their tropical homelands of Mexico, Brazil, and a number of Caribbean islands. Although they usually roost in tunnels or caves, they have occasionally been found under rock ledges (above).

might be the roosting site for bats representative of ten or more genera, with each type of bat preferring a particular perch.

Whatever the site, most bats hang upside down, with wings closed alongside their bodies, while roosting. A special arrangement of the leg tendons allows bats to assume and maintain this characteristic pose. It is an automatic grasp triggered and sustained by a weight pulling down on the flexor tendon. A force pulling down—in this case the weight of the bat's body—draws on the tendon, which in turn pulls the claw into a grasping position. A tendon sheath acts as a clamp, locking the tendon onto the toe bone and thereby securing the grip.

An equally appropriate adaptation allows some bats to roost in an upright position. The two species of the disc-winged family Thyropteridae are able to use suction pads at the base of each thumb and the ankles to maintain an upright position.

HIBERNATION

For many tropical species the site or type of roost is the same throughout the year. Because they are so close to the equator, abundant and constant food supplies and warm ambient temperatures eliminate the need for hibernation. Those living in temperate regions usually need to spend the winter in winter quarters. There they can spend the periods of diminished food supply in an extreme torpor that minimizes energy expenditure. The same temperature-regulating systems that allow full-scale hibernation are often employed while bats roost in warmer weather. Bats will often enter a state of torpor during the daytime. This state of reduced metabolic rate is much less extreme than hibernation but can still reduce energy expenditure by up to 75 percent.

There are key differences between roosting in summer and winter. An obvious difference is in social structure. Both sexes of many hibernating species spend the winter together, only to separate once spring arrives. During the summer they find different roosts, because pregnant and lactating females have more specific temperature and humidity needs. They reunite only when they are ready to breed again.

Among tropical species, males and females are more likely to roost together throughout the year. Some social structures emerge among these species, usually centering on a dominant male, although roosting patterns reflect a diversity of social structures, from monogamous pairs to colonies of millions. ■

REPRODUCTION

Bats reproduce in a seasonal cycle aligned to spring births in temperate climates or to the onset of rains in the tropics. They exhibit a range of mating patterns, from monogamy, as in white-lined bats, to harems, as in South American sac-winged and doglike bats. Males have a number of special skin glands that secrete territory-marking scents.

For hibernating species, the demands imposed by hibernation require different winter and summer roosting sites; a cool, damp winter roost is incompatible with the warmth needed by growing offspring. So female bats must build up enough fat reserves to nourish a developing fetus during hibernation. It is important, too, that the young be born in spring, when food is abundant. Bats have evolved a successful method of delayed fertilization so that the young are born at this time.

Pregnant females in many species form maternity colonies, usually in the warm, humid areas of a roost. In most species the female gives birth during the day. She hangs upside down during the birth, after which she frees the infant from the fetal membranes, severing the umbilical cord with her teeth. A few species give birth upright, in which case the mother supports herself on her thumb claws.

IN THE CRECHE

Young horseshoe bats hang up with other infants, waiting for their mothers to return (right). *Each female identifies her youngster among the heaving throng by the unique sound of its cries.*

MATING

Horseshoe bats mate in autumn (below), *but the fertilized ovum is not implanted until the next spring.*

Illustration Peter Beresford/Wildlife Art Agency

in SIGHT

TILL DEATH DO US PART

African yellow-winged bats, native to much of central Africa, live in permanent territorial pairs. Zoologists suggest that this monogamy is an evolutionary response to recurring periods of low food availability. This particular species is almost always associated with acacia trees because of the insects that are attracted when the acacias are in flower.

Births take place at the start of the long rainy season, when acacias are not in flower. The young bat clings to its mother as she forages, but the father maintains constant contact with them, roosting no more than 3 feet (a meter) from the mother and driving away other bat intruders from the territory. Indeed, the yellow-winged bats will prey on other bat species that try to share their habitat.

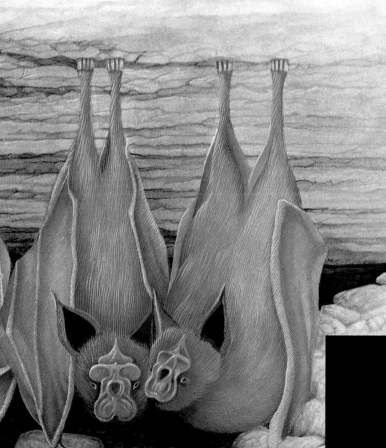

FROM BIRTH TO DEATH

GREATER HORSESHOE BAT	GREATER MOUSE-TAILED BAT
GESTATION: 7 WEEKS	**GESTATION:** ABOUT 17 WEEKS
LITTER SIZE: 1	**LITTER SIZE:** 1
BREEDING: AUTUMN (FERTILIZATION IN EARLY SPRING)	**BREEDING:** MARCH
WEIGHT AT BIRTH: 0.07–0.1 oz (2–3 G)	**WEIGHT AT BIRTH:** THOUGHT TO BE 15–20 PERCENT OF ADULT WEIGHT
FIRST FLIGHT: 3–4 WEEKS	**FIRST FLIGHT:** 3 WEEKS
WEANING: 6–8 WEEKS	**WEANING:** 6–8 WEEKS
SEXUAL MATURITY: 2 YEARS	**SEXUAL MATURITY:** SECOND YEAR OF LIFE
LONGEVITY: 6–7 NORMALLY, RARELY UP TO 25 YEARS	**LONGEVITY:** 3–4 YEARS

A lesser horseshoe bat nurses her young in the warm, moist conditions of a Spanish cave (below).

A young of some bat species clamp their teeth to the mother's teats, further anchoring themselves by digging their claws into her fur. Mothers will often fly about with young clinging to them in this fashion. Female horseshoe bats have an additional two false teats on their abdomen; these act as extra handles for offspring while the mother is in flight. When the young bats become heavier, they are left behind for longer periods while the mother resumes her normal hunting pattern.

There is a sense of shared maternal duty in the huge colonies of New World free-tailed bats. In colonies numbering in the millions, it would be impossible for each mother to locate and suckle her own offspring. So females returning from hunting simply suckle the young bats closest to them.

The body temperature of very young bats rises and falls with the ambient temperature, but they gradually develop the ability to maintain a steady temperature. By one month they are as successful as adults in this respect, and they can fly at about the same time. Independence follows with the end of weaning about a month after, with full sexual maturity reached at about fifteen months or later. ■

Antonio Manzanares/Bruce Coleman Ltd.

A LEGACY OF PERSECUTION

AMONG ALL THE WILD INHABITANTS OF THE HOME, BATS ARE AS MUCH MALIGNED AS SPIDERS—DESPITE THEIR INSECT-CONTROLLING BENEFITS. INDEED, BATS ARE UNIVERSALLY DISLIKED AND ARE WIDELY THREATENED

B ats face a number of threats to their survival, almost all of which can be traced to humans. Part of the problem lies in the low esteem in which bats are held. As nocturnal creatures, bats have traditionally been associated with darkness, even in the figurative sense. Lurid tales of blood sucking fuel this distaste and superstition. As a result, direct attacks on bats and their habitats are common throughout their wide range, regardless of whether the bats are pests, harmless, or even beneficial.

More systematic is the destruction of summer and winter roosting sites. When a householder discovers bats in the attic, his or her first reaction is usually one of disgust, followed rapidly by an attempt to evict the intruders. Even the partial loss of summer roosting sites can cause bat populations to scatter into smaller, isolated groups. The destruction of winter roosting sites—especially those of hibernating species—is even more threatening. Such sites must meet exacting requirements of darkness, humidity, and temperature; replacements are hard to find. The sites need not even be destroyed in order to lose their usefulness to bats.

Occasional disturbances can also be devastating to a hibernating bat colony. Even in their hibernating state, bats instinctively wake up when disturbed by a sudden noise or light. Waking up requires energy, which means that fatty deposits are burned up more rapidly than in the torpid state. Sometimes even one unexpected disturbance will cause a bat to use up its "fuel supply" before its normal wakening in spring. The result is fatal. In Britain and in some other countries it is illegal to seek out bat roosts.

CHEMICAL WARFARE

Intensive agriculture presents another systematic threat to bats. The more widespread use of chemicals—coupled with the introduction of more potent chemicals in developed countries—affects bats indirectly and directly. Farmers in Europe and in other developed regions rarely see bats as a threat, but their use of insecticides has led to drastic reductions in bat populations. The chemicals destroy the insects so effectively that the bats are deprived of their traditional food source. The figures are alarming for the free-tailed bats that colonize the caves of the southwestern United States and northern Mexico in the millions. The population in Eagles Creek, Arizona, one of several roosting sites studied over several decades, fell from 25–50 million in 1936 to 600,000 by 1970. Long-lasting pesticides, such as DDT, were blamed for this decline. DDT, which has a

H. Clark/Frank Lane Picture Agency

Iron grilles keep intruders from roost sites. Sadly, this one has been vandalized (above).

Matthias Breiter/Oxford Scientific Films

This map shows the former and current range of the Australian false vampire bat, also known as the ghost bat.

FORMER RANGE

CURRENT RANGE

The Australian false vampire or ghost bat, *Macroderma gigas*, is the largest of all insect-eating bats, with a wingspan of up to 23.5 in (60 cm). It roosts in caves and preys on rodents, birds, frogs, insects, and other bats. It was once widespread over Australia as far as 34° south. Today, as a result of increased aridity and disturbance from mining and quarrying concerns, its range extends only to about 29° south.

destructive effect on many wild species, is now banned in the United States but is still used in northern Mexico, where the bats spend the winter.

Fruit bats, on the other hand, are often considered to be pests in their own right, particularly to agriculture. There again, the blameless insectivorous bats have suffered. Large-scale fumigation of fruit bat roosting sites has also wiped out many local populations of insectivorous bats. In Israel, for example, Blasius's horseshoe bat is particularly at risk from this treatment.

A similar shotgun approach has been taken against vampire bats, which Latin American public health authorities have singled out as a threat to humans. Unfortunately their means of dealing with vampire bats are not focused on the three species in

Today the Australian ghost bat is protected by law, but is nevertheless still listed as vulnerable.

question. Instead, whole cave systems have been fumigated, wiping out roosting colonies of harmless —and even beneficial—insectivorous species. Moreover, these tactics have so far failed to reduce overall populations of vampire bats.

Loss of forest and woodland habitats is a concern across the world, threatening overall populations and endangering some unique species. Logging is the threat faced by the single species of the Myzopodidae family, the sucker-footed bat. This is the only bat family found solely on the island of Madagascar. The sucker-footed bat is superficially similar to the disc-winged bats of the New World, having sucker discs at the end of each thumb and ankle, but these discs are less efficiently utilized. Little is known about this species, which faces an uncertain future unless Madagascar adopts more effective controls upon the destruction of its forests.

INDIRECT THREATS

Some of the worst threats that bats face are indirect and insidious, sometimes only recognized well after the worst damage has been done. The decline of greater horseshoe bats in Europe has been well documented. Environmentalists and conservationists

---

IT IS AGAINST THE LAW IN BRITAIN TO DISTURB OR HARM BATS IN THE HOME; EXPERT ADVICE MUST BE SOUGHT

---

can rightly blame urban expansion and the suburbs spreading out from European cities. These factors have greatly reduced the summer and winter roosting sites of horseshoe bats. But only recently has a less obvious reason been put forward. Changes in farming practice have reduced the amount of pasture where a major food source, the dung beetle, once thrived. The land has retained its "green" function—at least at first glance—but the microhabitat has been changed permanently.

Mining is a serious threat to bats, largely because of its use of explosives in ore extraction. While destroying many bat roosting sites outright, explosives create shock and sound waves that render neighboring sites useless. There is also widespread use of toxic chemicals in ore extraction. Some mines in the United States still use cyanide in the gold-extraction process.

Linked with the problem of destruction of natural roosting sites, such as caves and woodlands, is the modification of "constructed" sites. New techniques, coupled with materials used in building modification and renovation, have affected bats. Attics once provided bats with ideal roosting sites. Old-fashioned attics were dark and cool, and

Jens Rydell/Bruce Coleman Ltd. Inset Hugh Aldridge/Planet Earth Pictures

ENDANGERED SPECIES

THE GREATER HORSESHOE BAT

The greater horseshoe bat has become emblematic of the problems facing many bat species. It occupies a number of natural and artificial habitats, in summer roosting in roofs, barns, and church belfries. In winter this species migrates more than 36 miles (60 km) to cool, damp roosting sites such as caves and mines. Some of these sites have been occupied for several hundred years.

Once widespread and common across Europe, the greater horseshoe bat has declined drastically. The figures are starkest in Britain, Belgium, Luxembourg, and Germany, but that probably reflects the level of study in those countries—colonies are threatened across the whole continent.

The reason for this decline is described impersonally as "habitat modification." In reality this modification means destruction of roosting sites and populations of insect prey. Urban development and vandalism have destroyed many artificial roosting areas, while the increased agricultural use of insecticides has decimated the traditional food supplies.

One problem lies with the greater horseshoe bat's habit of wrapping its wings entirely around its body while hanging up—many other bats simply fold their wings. This has the advantage of providing the bat with an "overcoat" that easily sheds any water droplets falling from the roof of a clammy cave. Unfortunately, it also exposes an excessive amount of

CONSERVATION MEASURES

● All bats in Britain are protected under the Wildlife and Countryside Act of 1981 and its 1988 amendment. The act includes a shortlist of threatened mammals, which is known as Schedule Five: This includes such species as the red squirrel, pine marten, otter, wildcat, and common dormouse, as well as all cetaceans (whales and dolphins). Under the act, it is an offense "intentionally to kill, injure or take a Schedule Five mammal that is free-living at the time." It is stipulated that wing, and the membranes act rather like a wick to evaporate body moisture. The hibernating bat needs to preserve precious fluids, and for this reason greater horseshoe bats are found mainly in winter quarters where the relative humidity is extremely high. Before its roosts were so wantonly altered, there were plenty of such sites to choose from. Today, however, its options are limited.

Statistics show that the greater horseshoe's population in England has suffered a 98 percent decline over the last century. A recent count estimated the population at around 2,200. The species is already extinct in the Netherlands and in Poland.

INSECT-EATING BATS IN DANGER

GRAY BAT	ENDANGERED
SEYCHELLES SHEATH-TAILED BAT	ENDANGERED
GEELVINCK BAY LEAF-NOSED BAT	RARE
KITTI'S HOG-NOSED BAT	RARE
GHOST BAT	VULNERABLE
GREATER MOUSE-EARED BAT	VULNERABLE
INDIANA BAT	VULNERABLE
LESSER SHORT-TAILED BAT	VULNERABLE
LONG-FINGERED BAT	VULNERABLE
POND BAT	VULNERABLE
RIDLEY'S LEAF-NOSED BAT	VULNERABLE
SUCKER-FOOTED BAT	VULNERABLE
WROUGHTON'S FREE-TAILED BAT	VULNERABLE
TOWNSEND'S BIG-EARED BAT	INDETERMINATE
GREATER SHEATH-TAILED BAT	INSUFFICIENTLY KNOWN
JAVAN THICK-THUMBED BAT	INSUFFICIENTLY KNOWN
JAVAN MASTIFF BAT	INSUFFICIENTLY KNOWN
RAFFRAY'S SHEATH-TAILED BAT	INSUFFICIENTLY KNOWN
ORANGE LEAF-NOSED BAT	INSUFFICIENTLY KNOWN

THE GREATER HORSESHOE BAT NEEDS MOIST HIBERNATION SITES—THESE ARE NOW SCARCE.

the word *intentionally* includes any actions undertaken with no regard to their effect. More pertinent to bats is the clause that adds that damaging, destroying, or obstructing access to a place or structure that is being used by a Schedule Five species for shelter or protection is an offense. Where bats are concerned, this clause is actionable even within the home—as testified by several successful prosecutions.

allowed access from outside. New buildings take into account modern concerns about heat loss—false floors, thick insulation, controlled ventilation, and good roofing ensure that their attics are too warm and dry for effective bat hibernation. Loft conversions also rule out hibernation.

Renovations and timber renewal can also harm bats. Wood preservatives containing chlorinated hydrocarbons such as lindane or PCP are often the culprits. They are soluble in fat, which means they are not hazardous in periods when bats have built up fat reserves. The trouble comes when these fats have been dispersed through the bat's body, causing concentrations of the toxic substances to increase in the remaining fat and elsewhere in the body. Results can be fatal if enough substances build up in the brain. The high fat solubility also means that these toxic substances can be passed on to offspring through lactation.

WHEN GOOD INTENTIONS FAIL

Sometimes human intervention is well intentioned but still detrimental to bat welfare. A case in point concerns the golden horseshoe bat, native to northern Australia. This species roosts in hot, humid conditions, with relative humidity reaching 100 percent at times. The largest known colony, at Cutta Cutta Cave in the Northern Territory, numbered about 5,000 bats in 1966. Local authorities covered the cave entrance with a mesh grille, which was meant to keep inquisitive tourists out but to allow bats to enter. This attempt failed, since bats also found themselves barred from entry, and only a few

Mike Brown/Oxford Scientific Films

hundred survived. The grille was removed, and other methods now mark the cave as strictly "off limits" to humans. The bat population has increased, but it is still less than half of its level 30 years ago.

Ironically, some of the worst bat disruption stems from misguided scientific studies. There is now a moratorium on banding or tagging bats in the United States; earlier studies used these techniques to monitor bat populations and their movements. Sadly, they met with limited success, and many bats were injured or distressed in the process. It must also be remembered that a scientific party can disrupt a bat roosting site as effectively as a vandal.

The effect of these human threats can easily be compounded by a bat species' physiology. For example, spending a great deal of time aloft imposes a number of constraints on bats. As with birds, their bodies have evolved in a way that minimizes weight and emphasizes aerodynamics. But whereas bats, as mammals, are usually thought of as more "advanced" animals, birds have an advantage in one area—breeding. Females can fly unhampered by their developing young, which remain ground-based as eggs or nestlings.

A female bat, however, is burdened with the fetus inside her; this has two consequences. One is that multiple births are extremely rare—the weight of one extra passenger is quite enough. The other is that bats make up for this low seasonal birth rate by breeding over a long period. Many bats live for twenty years or more—unless, of course, their nursery and winter roosts are disturbed or destroyed outright or they have been poisoned with wood preservatives or pesticides. ■

With their stable conditions, edifices such as this Cambodian temple provide ideal roost sites.

Lesser mouse-tailed bats (above) *roost in large colonies in caves, houses, wells, and even pyramids or tombs.*

ALONGSIDE MAN

AN IMAGE PROBLEM

To a medieval European, there were few terrors greater than what seemed to be a flying rat, an animal that lurked in graveyards and crypts. No one imagined that bats were in fact helpful, ridding farms of insect pests. Instead, bats became linked with the dead—or even worse, the undead.

Fear about bats continued long after the "Age of Reason" (1660–1780). Bats were featured in Gustave Doré's illustrations of Dante's *Inferno* and were central to *Dracula*. Darwin was promoting his *Origin of Species*, chemical elements were being discovered, and physics was undergoing sweeping changes. Yet new life was being breathed into bat myths.

We are not immune from such idle superstition. Think of the decorations for a children's Halloween party. There are witches, brooms, pumpkins, and ghosts, but what animals keep the black cats company?

Michael Freeman/Bruce Coleman Ltd.

INTO THE FUTURE

Bats face an uncertain future worldwide. Most species live in the insect-rich tropics, where the human problems of underdevelopment and overpopulation work against bats. Apart from the direct attacks, caused by ignorance or as side effects of measures controlling "pest" species, there is a huge problem of habitat destruction. Forestry, mining, intensive agriculture, and cave tourism are often seen as crucial for generating foreign currency. They also ruin natural hunting and roosting sites for bats. Gradual declines seem to be inevitable.

But there is some cause for optimism. "Green" issues have risen to the top of the political agenda in many countries, prompting politicians, farmers,

PREDICTION

THE COST OF DEVELOPMENT
Increased "green" awareness in the developed world just might bring some temperate-climate species back from the brink of extinction. Bats in the tropics will fare less well; overall declines are still predicted, with BCI (see box) estimating that up to 120 species are probably endangered.

urban planners, and developers to appreciate animal concerns. Legislation such as Britain's 1981 Wildlife and Countryside Act has already helped matters.

Bats also benefit from some of the more wide-ranging agricultural measures throughout the European Community and in the United States. Europeans have reversed a trend typified by the Common Agricultural Policy, which encouraged the conversion of wetlands and scrub into farmland. New legislation offers financial incentives for preserving existing woodlands, wetlands, and grasslands.

Measures are being taken in Germany and elsewhere in Europe to monitor and protect summer roosting sites in cities. These efforts combine with the work of volunteers and environmental authorities, who advise about building materials and the best season in which to renovate or build houses. Artificial roosting boxes are sometimes installed in areas where natural sites have been lost.

Some of these measures are being introduced in less developed countries, but two problems hinder their wider use. One is proving that conservation measures need not bring about a necessary economic trade-off; the other is finding the funds for their implementation in the first place. ■

WORLDWIDE SUPPORT

International environmental organizations can play a leading role in promoting conservation and, equally important, in helping overcome widely held misconceptions about bats.

Bat Conservation International (BCI) has set itself both of these goals, with an obvious concentration on bat welfare. Founded in Austin, Texas, in 1982, it now has members in more than fifty countries. The international nature of the organization helps BCI to promote a wide range of bat-protection measures. These include, on a basic level, promotion of bat conservation programs worldwide. BCI also offers sensible, cost-effective advice on how to control vampire bats and fruit bats without harming beneficial insectivorous species. Fruit bats can pose particular problems for fruit farmers, since a single bat colony can strip an orchard overnight. Much of BCI's literature is also printed in Spanish, making it more useful for on-site application throughout Latin America. BCI has bought a number of roosting sites outright, as the ultimate guarantee against disturbance.

Illustration Wildlife Art Agency

ROOST PROTECTION

The protection of bats' roosting sites is crucial to their survival, and Britain's Wildlife and Countryside Act of 1981 is typical of the legislated approach to conservation. It prohibits direct attacks on bats and severely restricts handling of any bat species. More hard-hitting are the bans on any attempts to disturb a roosting site or to disturb bats themselves while roosting. Such wide-ranging legislation does not shirk from imposing restrictions on how home owners and churches maintain their own properties.

VESPER BATS

RELATIONS

Vesper bats belong to the immense bat suborder Microchiroptera, which includes:

MOUSE-TAILED BATS

SHEATH-TAILED BATS

SLIT-FACED BATS

VAMPIRE BATS

BULLDOG BATS

SPEAR-NOSED BATS

DISC-WINGED BATS

Wendy Shattil/Bob Rozinski/Oxford Scientific Films

The vesper bats (or common bats) are the largest family in the bat suborder Microchiroptera: the insectivorous or carnivorous bats characterized by their sonar hunting and navigation technique. There are a total of 18 families in the suborder; the remaining bat family, the Pteropodidae, consists of the large, fruit-eating flying foxes that navigate by sight, and is classified in the suborder Megachiroptera.

NIGHT RAIDERS

SUPERBLY EQUIPPED FOR PURSUING THEIR INSECT PREY THROUGH THE NIGHT SKY, THE VESPER BATS ARE AMONG THE MOST EXQUISITELY ADAPTED OF ALL MAMMALS

ORDER

Chiroptera
(bats)

SUBORDER

Microchiroptera
(largely
insectivorous bats)

FAMILY

Vespertilionidae
(vesper bats)

42 GENERA

355 SPECIES

I magine your hands are wings. Hold them out before you and visualize the fingers extending until they are each as long as your arm. Web them with dark, supple membranes of skin, held taut by slender muscle fibers, stretched from fingertip to fingertip and fingertip to ankle. Move them slowly through the air; feel the resistance and the cool swirl of the current. Beat them down hard and feel them grip the air in handfuls, caught by the webs of dark skin

and muscle. Feel the tendons tighten as, hauling down on the thick, fluid air, your body leaps into the sky. Feel what it is to be a bat.

A bat flies with its hands. Unlike a bird's wing, which is tiled with stiff-quilled feathers sprouting from a fleshy forelimb, a bat's wing is supported entirely by the long bones of the arm and hand. The word *chiroptera*, used to describe the entire order of bats, means "hand-winged." The evolution of such a structure is easier to understand than the

211

wing of a bird, but maybe this is because bats are mammals and their basic anatomy is more like our own. Consequently the series of adaptations that has given bats the power of flight seems almost too straightforward compared to the feathered complexity of birds, and bats are generally assumed to be relatively poor fliers. Yet while bats cannot fly as fast or as high as birds, the smaller species are far more agile in the air, and in their own way the bats are at least as successful as the birds.

MOST SUCCESSFUL MAMMALS

Their success can be measured by their sheer variety. Bats comprise a quarter of all the mammal species alive today, with some 950 species scientifically identified. The vast majority are insect-eaters in the suborder Microchiroptera. Like the primitive mammals from which they evolved, their teeth and digestive systems are relatively unspecialized. This has encouraged intense competition for prey, forcing the pace of evolution by putting a premium on any adaptation that confers an advantage in any specific set of circumstances. The result is the huge variety of species, many of which are so similar that only an expert can tell them apart.

A third of these, at least 319 species, share enough features to be classified in the same family: Vespertilionidae (ves-per-tih-lee-ON-id-eye), or vesper bats. The name is derived from the evening church service of vespers and refers to their habit of appearing at dusk. Vespertilionidae is the biggest of the bat families, the least specialized, and the most widely distributed. The genus *Myotis,* which accounts for 97 species in the family, is the least

Stephen Dalton/NHPA

Melvin Gray/NHPA

As its name suggests, the common long-eared bat (above) *has outsize ears that touch at the base.*

212

SAVING ENERGY

The object of a bat's enhanced maneuverability is to enable it to capture insects in flight. Vesper bats are nearly all aerial hunters, with highly developed senses for detecting and pinpointing their prey in the dark. This gives them a virtual monopoly on an abundant food supply in the warmer months, but in temperate latitudes it exposes them to the risk of starvation when insects are scarce in winter. Prey may even be hard to find in high summer on rainy, windy, or cold days, and since small, active mammals like bats burn a lot of energy when they are active, this is potentially disastrous. Their solution is to conserve energy by lying dormant throughout most of the winter and during periods when they cannot hunt, allowing their body temperature to fall to the point where the metabolic rate is reduced.

specialized of all the vespertilionid genera and occurs worldwide with the exception of the polar regions and a few islands. It has the widest distribution of any land mammal apart from humans.

The origins of this immensely successful group of animals are obscure. In the case of bats the earliest remains found so far—a skeleton dating from the early Eocene epoch of some 50 million years ago—are very like those of modern bats, complete with highly developed wings, so the early stages in the evolution of these flying mammals remain a mystery. Eocene bats have been found with the remains of moth scales in their stomachs, suggesting that they had already acquired the ability to catch nocturnal insects in flight.

Rocks from the early Oligocene epoch, about 35 million years ago, contain the remains of bats belonging to many of the modern families, including the Vespertilionidae, and some bones dating from this epoch are virtually identical to those of modern species. This is remarkable considering that at this time horses, for example, had yet to evolve beyond three-toed creatures the size of goats. Clearly bats have been around for a very long time, and the first may have taken to the air before the extinction of the dinosaurs some 65 million years ago.

Powered flight is what distinguishes bats from all other mammals, including the so-called flying

Vesper bats, such as the mouse-eared bat, are designed for maximum maneuverability in the air.

squirrels and flying lemurs, which are actually only capable of gliding. All these airborne mammals have adopted the same device: a membrane of skin and muscle called a patagium, which in flight is stretched between outspread limbs to form a type of wing. In the gliding mammals, the wing is relatively unsophisticated, but in bats the elongated finger bones support the patagium in a classic airfoil profile that creates lift as the bat moves forward through the air. When the bat is gliding, the whole wing takes up this profile, but in powered flight the wings are swept down by muscles attached to the bat's breastbone and ribs, and the flexible trailing edges of the outer sections of the webs between the finger bones are distorted upward by the pressure. In this condition they push the air backward like the blades of a propeller, providing the power that propels the bat through the night sky.

AERODYNAMIC AND AGILE

The aerodynamics of bats are tailored for highly maneuverable flight, and some of the vesper bats are among the most agile of all. Their impermeable wing membranes allow for much tighter turns than the separate wing feathers of birds. The hind limbs are so weak that they are incapable of supporting the bat in a normal upright posture, and this is one reason why bats generally hang upside down at the roost. Weight is saved in the wings themselves by concentrating the active flight muscles at the wing roots. The outer sections, the fingers, are operated by "remote control" through slender, inelastic muscles that unfurl automatically when the inner sections, the arms, are extended. When the wings are folded in to the sides of the bat's body, the finger sections are automatically folded up. As soon as the wings are folded, the bat slips into standby mode— "switched off" to save valuable energy. ∙ ■

Color illustrations Steve Kingston

Despite the lack of comprehensive fossil evidence, zoologists have classified the microchiropteran bats into four superfamilies (see box). These superfamilies provide a convenient grouping, but their scientific validity is still in doubt. New fossil evidence may suggest affinities between bats in different superfamilies, and modern protein analysis may reveal previously unsuspected relationships between existing species. Entirely new species are still being discovered.

COMMON PIPISTRELLE

Pipistrellus pipistrellus
(pih-pih-STRELL-us pih-pih-STRELL-us)

One of the smallest of the vesper bats, the common pipistrelle is typical of these relatively adaptable insect-eaters, which in general are equipped for catching **prey in the air using echolocation. It is the most frequently seen bat in northern Europe, since it is common in towns, where it often roosts in the eaves and roof spaces of new houses.**

FRUIT BATS (MEGACHIROPTERA)

SHEATH-TAILED BAT SUPERFAMILY EMBALLONUROIDAE

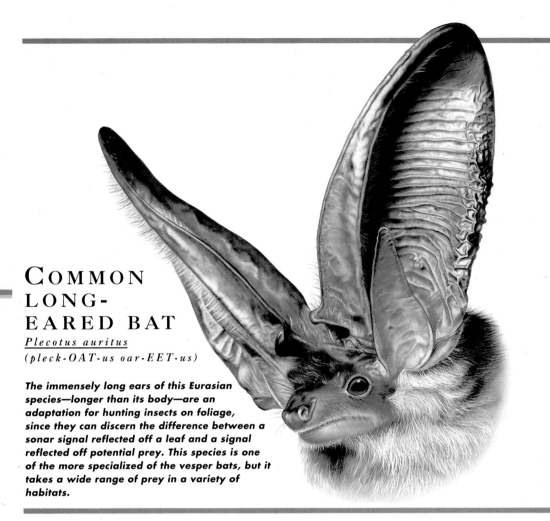

COMMON LONG-EARED BAT

Plecotus auritus
(pleck-OAT-us oar-EET-us)

The immensely long ears of this Eurasian species—longer than its body—are an adaptation for hunting insects on foliage, since they can discern the difference between a sonar signal reflected off a leaf and a signal reflected off potential prey. This species is one of the more specialized of the vesper bats, but it takes a wide range of prey in a variety of habitats.

HORSESHOE BAT
SUPERFAMILY RHINOLOPHOIDEA

LEAF-NOSED BATS
SUPERFAMILY PHYLLOSTOMATOIDEA

SUPERFAMILIES

The microchiropterans are grouped into four superfamilies, mainly on the basis of physical structure. The vesper bats form the basis of the Vespertilionoidea superfamily; grouped with them are the free-tailed bats, funnel-eared bats, disc-winged bats, thumbless bats, and sucker-footed bats. The other three superfamilies are the leaf-nosed bats and their allies, the Phyllostomatoidea; the horseshoe bats and their allies, the Rhinolophoidea; and the sheath-tailed bats and their allies, the Emballonuroidae.

B/W illustrations Ruth Grewcock/Sheath-tailed bat Chris Christoforou

ANATOMY: THE PIPISTRELLE BAT

The pipistrelle is tiny, much smaller than a mouse, with a head-and-body length of less than 2 in (50 mm), but its wingspan extends to 10 in (250 mm).

THE FUR

is dense and long, making the bat look much plumper than it really is. The bat grooms its fur regularly and thoroughly with its hind feet, keeping it meticulously clean, and it is molted and replaced every year.

THE EARS

are smaller than those of many bats, yet highly sensitive to high-pitched sounds and the ultrasonic sonar echoes reflected from obstacles and flying insects.

THE EYES

work perfectly well, but they cannot distinguish color because they are adapted for high sensitivity in low light levels rather than color reception.

B/W illustration Ruth Grewcock

VESPER BAT'S FACE
The faces of vesper bats are more appealing than those of many insectivorous bats. Typical species like the mouse-eared bat (left) have simple muzzles like hedgehogs.

X

R A Y

SKELETON
A bat has slender bones and small hind legs to minimize weight. All the strength of its skeleton is concentrated in its shoulders and the inner parts of its wings. The outer wing is supported by the elongated finger bones. It has movable collarbones and shoulder blades for greater maneuverability.

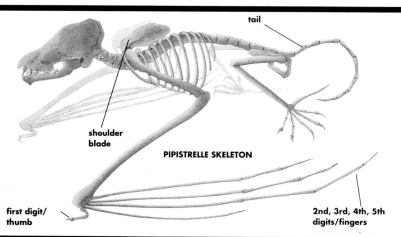

tail

shoulder blade

PIPISTRELLE SKELETON

first digit/ thumb

2nd, 3rd, 4th, 5th digits/fingers

SKULL
The shape of the skull of the different vesper bat species varies depending on their diet. Those bats that eat hard-shelled insects, such as beetles, have a shorter, broader muzzle and may have a more domed head. The skulls of species, such as the pipistrelle, that feed on moths and flies, are flatter and more elongated, with a longer, narrower muzzle.

X-ray illustrations Elisabeth Smith

EAR SHAPES

Most vesper bats have big ears that are equipped with an extra lobe called the tragus. The massive ears of the barbastelle (right) dominate its broad, puglike face, and those of the long-eared bat (far right) are longer than its body.

BARBASTELLE BAT

COMMON LONG-EARED BAT

FACT FILE

COMMON PIPISTRELLE

CLASSIFICATION

GENUS: *PIPISTRELLUS*

SPECIES: *PIPISTRELLUS*

SIZE

HEAD–BODY LENGTH: 1.25–1.75 IN (35–45 MM)

WINGSPAN: 7.5–10 IN (190–250 MM)

WEIGHT: 0.1–0.3 OZ (3–8 G)

WEIGHT AT BIRTH: 0.03–0.06 OZ (1–2 G)

COLORATION

DARK BROWN ABOVE, PALER BELOW; BROWN-BLACK WING MEMBRANES, EARS, AND FEET. YOUNG ARE PINK.

FEATURES

TINY BODY WITH THICK, BROWN FUR

RELATIVELY SHORT, BROAD EARS

SMALL, BROWN EYES

"NORMAL" NOSE

WELL-DEVELOPED TAIL MEMBRANE WITH PROTRUDING TAIL

THE TAIL

is roughly half as long as the bat's body and supports a membrane stretched between the two hind legs. The last joint of the tail is free and prehensile, and the bat uses it as a support as it crawls around.

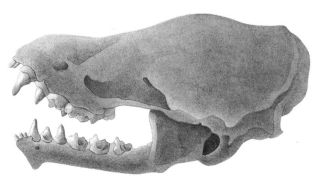

THE HIND FEET

have sharp claws capable of gripping the slightest irregularity in a wall or timber beam. As the bat hangs upside down, its weight pulls down on a special arrangement of tendons that tighten the grip, ensuring it does not fall off as it sleeps.

THE WINGS

re formed from two heets of skin andwiching a layer of lastic tissue and muscle ibers. They are upported by the longated arm and inger bones.

THE HIND LEGS

are short and slender and, as with all bats, they are turned "back to front," so they bend forward below the knee.

PIPISTRELLE SKULL

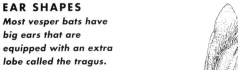

TEETH

Many vesper bats have powerful jaws and strong, pointed teeth for catching and killing well-armored insects and even small vertebrates, such as lizards and fish. The front incisors are often missing, leaving a gap in the center of the jaw. The hard, zigzag cusps on the cheek teeth make short work of crunching up the bat's victims.

SKULL OF *EPTESICUS*
(top section looking up)

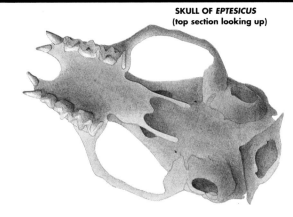

Main illustration Guy Troughton/Wildlife Art Agency

SONAR HUNTERS

ALTHOUGH THEY ARE AMONG THE MOST EFFICIENT HUNTERS IN THE ANIMAL WORLD, MANY VESPER BATS SPEND MUCH OF THEIR LIVES ON THE BRINK OF STARVATION, AT THE MERCY OF CLIMATIC CONDITIONS

As the summer light softens at dusk, swarms of tiny flies swirl up into the sky. They are easy prey for the swifts that swoop down to trawl up a late meal. Larger flying insects attract another predator, which darts with equal skill on long, scalloped wings—a noctule bat. Long after the swifts have faded into the night, the noctule will still be probing for its invisible prey.

By day the birds rule the skies, using their eyes to home in on prey, but this technique is of little use at night. Yet in summer the night sky is often full of mosquitoes, moths, and beetles, offering a feast for any animal capable of catching them. This opportunity has been exploited by bats.

Nearly all the vesper bats are nocturnal aerial hunters. The pallid bat snatches its victims from the ground, and the long-eared bats can pluck prey off foliage, but such skills are basically refinements of the hunting technique that has given bats mastery of the night sky. The basis of this technique is echolocation: a sound-based sensory system that enables bats to "see" in the dark.

EYES IN THE NIGHT

A vesper bat uses its flight muscles to generate a stream of high-pitched sound pulses and uses its specialized hearing to monitor the echoes reflected by any objects in its vicinity. The echo delay (the interval between the emission and reception of the pulse) and the nature of the received signal define the range, size, and even texture of nearby objects, and the bat's keen sense of stereophony registers their exact location. The constant stream of information is computed within the bat's brain, which creates an image of its surroundings—an image that probably matches the information gathered by the eyes. The difference, of course, is that it works equally well in any light.

But this "sonar" system functions only at short range. In good visibility most animals can see to the horizon and spot prey from afar. But a bat using sonar is only aware of the immediate vicinity. The system's long-range performance can be improved: The louder the signal, and the lower its frequency, the further it will travel, and many bats emit very loud pulses—although these are still too high for us to hear. High-flying species like the noctule use long, low-frequency pulses to boost their sonar range. But in general, vespers use short, high-frequency pulses for better image discrimination (to isolate small insects from large objects), and, as a result, they suffer from the sonar equivalent of nearsightedness.

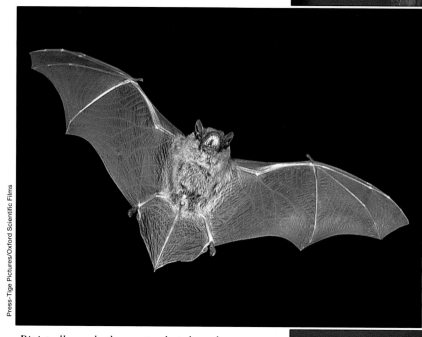

Pipistrelles and other vesper bats have been known to migrate over hundreds of miles (above).

Press-Tige Pictures/Oxford Scientific Films

Frank Scheidermeyer/Oxford Scientific Films

HANGING AROUND

All bats can hang upside down by the claws of their hind feet when resting. To us this seems odd, but to a bat it is ideal. It is out of reach of most predators, high above any puddles and debris, and can simply unhook itself and spread its wings to fly.

The bat's pin-sharp hind claws enable it to cling to a crevice as little as four thousandths of an inch deep. Once it has latched on, its own weight pulls on the tendons that draw the claws together, so as long as it relaxes, it will not fall; the bat actually has to make a special effort to let go. This means that simply roosting uses up no energy at all.

But hanging upside down is not without complications. Bats have had to evolve special valves and muscles in their blood vessels to prevent the blood from rushing to their heads, and if a bat needs to urinate it must unhook one claw and twist its body to one side to avoid a drenching.

This has a profound effect on bat's flight. A hunting bat—particularly a low-flying species like the pipistrelle—tends to swerve suddenly to avoid obstacles that have just come into focus, or careers off in pursuit of an insect that has passed through its field of perception. It looks haphazard, but since the bat's mobile shoulders and infinitely adjustable wings allow almost instant changes in direction, what looks like a sequence of near misses is more like a masterful display of aerobatics.

A WELL-EARNED BREAK

All this burns energy, of course, and a lot is wasted as heat radiated from the bat's wings. So when a bat is not hunting—which is most of the time—it normally slips into standby mode to save energy. This involves locating a secure, quiet roost, typically with other bats of the same species, finding a foothold, and hanging up in a state of suspended animation. As soon as the bat folds its wings, its body temperature begins to fall to match its surroundings. In hot weather it may not fall very far, and the bats in the roost may be restless and noisy throughout the day. But on dull, rainy days in northern latitudes the roosting bats slip into a deep torpor until some instinct arouses them to take to the air again in the gathering dusk. ■

Bats hang up after hunting, in order to reduce their metabolic rate and save precious energy.

HABITATS

Vesper bats have a vast range worldwide. As the least specialized of the bat families they are also the most adaptable, and they are found in every type of habitat, from tropical rain forest and desert to the Arctic tundra, wherever there are suitable roosting sites and adequate supplies of prey. The ability to fly long distances has enabled them to exploit habitats inaccessible to other mammals, such as islands, and it has also enabled them to spread quickly into new areas, sample what they have to offer, and either stay or move on as appropriate. In the past, for example, bats have been unable to exploit the teeming insect life on the Arctic tundra because there are few caves and no large trees to roost in, but the northern serotine has recently been able to colonize parts of Arctic Lapland because the building of houses has provided them with roosting sites.

I. & L. Beames/Ardea

THE COMMON PIPISTRELLE FLOURISHES IN A DIVERSITY OF HABITATS, FROM OAK FORESTS TO MODERN SUBDIVISIONS

The more opportunist the species, the broader its range of potential habitats. The common pipistrelle, for example, feeds on a wide variety of small flying insects, hunts over small areas, and is prepared to roost almost anywhere, including hollow trees, rock crevices, ruins, and occupied buildings. Its tiny frame enables it to slip through the smallest gaps, and pipistrelles often take up residence in newly built houses by creeping behind tile-hung facades, into wall cavities, beneath roof tiles, and under the eaves.

COPING WITH COMPETITION

In urban areas the pipistrelle has the nocturnal insect population to itself, but elsewhere it must compete with other bats for the same prey. Such an intense level of competition has encouraged many vesper bats to develop specialties and adaptations of their own, and while none of these are as extreme as those of, say, the nectar-feeding long-nosed bats, they have radically altered the habits of some species and effectively restricted them to certain habitats.

Among the most specially adapted of the vesper bats are the long-eared bats. There are several species, including the Eurasian and American long-eared bats of the genus *Plecotus,* the Australasian big-eared bats, and the spotted or

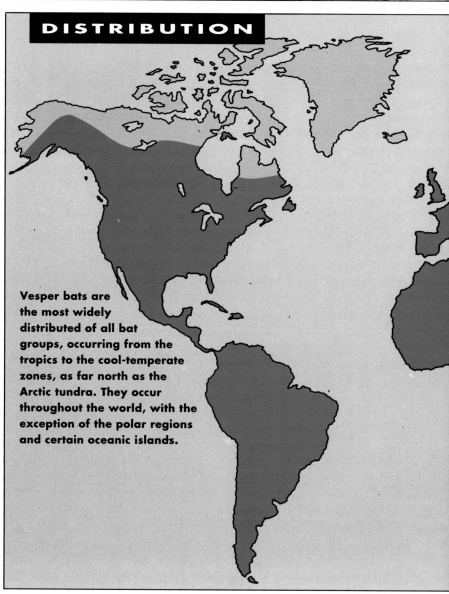

DISTRIBUTION

Vesper bats are the most widely distributed of all bat groups, occurring from the tropics to the cool-temperate zones, as far north as the Arctic tundra. They occur throughout the world, with the exception of the polar regions and certain oceanic islands.

The sight of a bat crawling awkwardly "on all fours" (left) emphasizes the fact that these animals are specially adapted for flight and for hanging up. Nevertheless, they can scuttle from a landing site to a perch, using the claws on their hands and feet.

KEY FACTS

● The summer roosts used by bats in temperate latitudes are not necessarily the same as the sites used for hibernation, because their temperature requirements are different. Nursery roosts in particular need to be warm if the newly born bats are to thrive, but hibernation sites must be cool and humid.

● Many roosting sites have been used for centuries, particularly by species that prefer caves. However, bats have been known to move into the roof spaces of new houses within a year of completion.

● Many bat species have a well-developed homing instinct, and bats that have been captured in houses, marked, and released far away often return to their original roost within a day or so. They probably navigate by sight on such journeys since echolocation is a short-range system, ideal for avoiding obstacles but ill-suited to route finding.

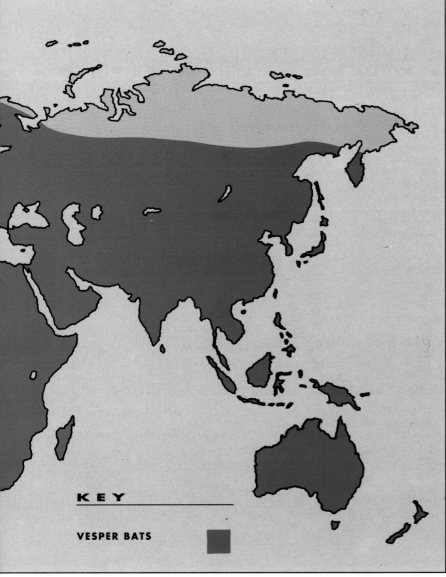

KEY

VESPER BATS ■

pinto bat of North America. These species have extrasensitive hearing, and in the case of *Plecotus* this is used in conjunction with a refined form of echolocation to find insects among the foliage of trees and bushes. Locating the victim is only half the job, however; the bat still has to catch it, and accordingly it has developed broad, high-lift wings that enable it to fly very slowly and even hover in tree foliage to pinpoint its target and slip in for the kill. These adaptations naturally predispose the long-eared bats to forested and wooded habitats, where they can exploit prey that is inaccessible to less perceptive, less agile species.

A similar combination of sensory discrimination and flying skill enables the pallid bat of North America to locate and catch large ground-dwelling insects, scorpions, and lizards. This involves flying low over the ground so that the bat's sonar equipment can pick out the prey's profile against the horizon. The technique is most effective in regions where the ground is barren, and accordingly the pallid bat typically occurs in desert areas (as does the quite unrelated African slit-faced bat, which has the same hunting habits).

Another low flyer is Daubenton's bat, a Eurasian species that skims low over rivers and lakes to snap up emerging mayflies, caddis flies, and other aquatic insects, flying with fast, shallow wing beats to get really close to the surface. It may even hook the odd fish, but of the vesper bats the real fishing specialist is the *Myotis vivesi*. This Mexican species is the nearest any bat comes to being a marine animal, for it roosts in coastal caves, cliff crevices, and in among boulders, emerging to hunt over the waters of Baja California and even the open Pacific; once a group of 400 or so were seen hunting around a boat at least 4.3 miles (7 km) from the coast.

SPECIAL ROOSTS

Some vesper bats are highly adapted to certain roost sites. The two bamboo bat species of Southeast Asia have flattened skulls, enabling them to slip through the slits in large bamboo stems made by emerging beetle larvae. Once inside, the bats roost in groups of up to 40 within the hollow stem, each hanging by circular suction pads on its feet and at the base of its thumbs.

The roosting sites of bats are generally close to their feeding habitats, but not always. Some cave-roosting species form colonies of up to a hundred thousand in summer (hibernation colonies in winter are often much bigger), largely because suitable caves are widely scattered; such a huge number of bats would rapidly destroy their food supply if they confined their hunting to their local area, so they commute between their roosting dormitories and widespread feeding sites.

Species that roost in trees or buildings have a wider choice of refuges and usually roost within easy flying distance of their prey, but a woodland

Michael Leach/Oxford Scientific Films

FOCUS ON

LIFE IN THE ATTIC

An undisturbed roof space is an ideal summer roost site for bats such as these brown long-eared bats. Warm and dry, with plenty of snug crevices, it makes a perfect nursery for the vulnerable newborn young. Provided the bats have easy access and the timber is not treated with insecticide, they may return year after year.

It is rare for more than one species to share a site. Large bats, such as serotines, need big access holes and are generally found in old, dilapidated buildings. Smaller species, such as the common long-eared bat, can squeeze through the gaps in well-maintained roofs, and pipistrelles actually seem to prefer recently built houses. But most of the vespertilionid bats prefer big, old houses with access holes and a variety of microclimates within the roof space. Bats have precise temperature preferences that alter with the seasons and even from day to day, and a colony will often move about as the sun heats up different parts of a big loft.

Bats prefer clean sites and avoid dusty corners. Most species form tight clusters between the rafters or behind boards. Several hundred may squeeze into a small space, and even large colonies may thrive quite unsuspected by the human inhabitants below.

COLONY NUMBERS

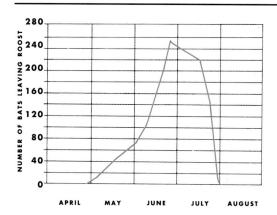

The particolored bat is a very unusual species in that the males gather in a single-sex colony during summer. From counts of flight numbers made at a German roost site, it can be seen that colony populations peak in June/July. After this, the males fly off to establish courtship sites.

hunter like the common long-eared bat may prefer to roost in a snug roof space rather than a drafty tree, even if it means a longer journey to its preferred feeding area. Such bats often adopt buildings as roosting sites simply because natural refuges such as hollow trees have become scarce, but suitable buildings are also becoming scarce as property owners become more conscientious about maintenance and repairs. As a result, many species are finding roosting sites increasingly hard to find and are disappearing from habitats where they were once abundant. ∎

NEIGHBORS

At first glance, attics may seem lifeless places—but for a few spiders perhaps. A suitable roof space, however, may be just the right residence for a surprisingly diverse array of animals.

GRAY SQUIRREL

Given the chance, this opportunist will set up home in a loft, building a football-sized nest of twigs.

COMMON WASP

Few attic residents are as unwelcome as wasps, but their paper nests are marvels of architecture.

Illustrations Evi Antoniou & Chris Christoforou

FAT (EDIBLE) DORMOUSE

The nocturnal fat dormouse often enters lofts and makes a nuisance of itself by scuttling about at night.

SWIFT

Although it spends most of its life feeding on the wing, the swift often nests on walls and in roof spaces.

HOUSE MOUSE

Since house mice feed on a wide variety of unlikely materials, they may thrive in attics used for storage.

HOUSE SPIDER

This is usually the species responsible for those large and dusty, hammocklike cobwebs in the attic.

JACKDAW

Jackdaws often breed in disused chimneys, which the birds stuff with sticks to support each nest.

HUNTING

Insects are tricky targets; few birds can catch them on the wing by day, let alone at night. But on any summer evening a small bat may locate, identify, and trap 500 insects an hour.

This is made possible by echolocation. A bat sweeping through a cloud of gnats may scoop them up by simply opening its mouth, but few insects swarm in such numbers. And while gnats may sustain a small bat, they could not satisfy larger bats. Moreover, each species has a specialized diet. So the large, fast noctule takes individual beetles, crickets, and large moths, leaving the smaller flies to pipistrelles and other small bats.

Emerging at sunset, all the bats in a colony usually follow the same flight path from the roost, then head off for their own favorite sites. Among pipistrelles, each bat adopts a regular patrol pattern, using trees or other features as landmarks. Most vesper bats probably use similar tactics. If the hunting is good, the bat may patrol for hours, and even defend its area as an exclusive feeding territory. Tickell's bat, a tropical Southeast Asian species, returns to the same beat each night and drives away any trespassers of the same species.

SOUNDING OUT THE TERRAIN

As it flies, a bat emits a barrage of ultrasonic calls, sweeping its head from side to side and monitoring the reflected echoes. On the flight from the roost the calls are loud but relatively infrequent because their main purpose is to prevent collision with large, solid objects. Each pulse corresponds to a wing beat, so when flying at a high altitude the noctule uses the power of its pumping flight muscles to call at a rate of one loud pulse per second to verify its height and surroundings. By contrast, a species like Daubenton's bat, which flies with rapid wing beats near the surfaces of lakes and rivers, calls at a rate of 13 pulses per second—a physical consequence of its rapid wing beats that also provides the constant stream of position information the bat needs to avoid disaster.

CLOSING IN FOR THE KILL

If the bat detects possible prey, it closes in rapidly, accelerating its calling rate far faster than the wing beat, using the frenzied buzz to sharpen the sound image. Meanwhile it follows every swerve of its quarry. Usually it catches it easily, either with its teeth or its tail membrane, but more agile insects may have to be fielded with a wing tip. Some moths can detect bat calls and escape by closing their wings and dropping at the critical moment. A tiger moth responds to a bat's pulses with calls of its own; these jam the bat's sonar, enabling the moth to escape in the confusion.

Caught insects are eaten in flight or, if they are large, taken to a perch to be dismembered. If the hunting is good, the bat may be back at the roost within an hour or two of sunset with a full stomach. This can increase its body weight by as much as 25 percent. But the food passes quickly through the digestive system, and, as dawn approaches, the bat will be back on patrol. ∎

HUNTING GROUNDS

Most bats have favorite feeding areas, such as along woodland edges, where flowers attract night-flying moths, or along rivers when the caddis flies and mayflies are hatching.

DRINKING ON THE WING

Although a bat gets most of its moisture from its insect prey, it does need to drink occasionally, particularly if its daytime roost is warmed by the sun. It may simply land near a pond or stream and creep over to lap up some water, but many bats drink on the wing. A common pipistrelle, for example, skims over the surface of a pool like a swallow, dipping its lower jaw to scoop up a stream of water. It may do this several times before its thirst is satisfied. Usually bats are graceful, precise drinkers, but occasionally pipistrelles land in the water—presumably by mistake, since they cannot take off again and must use their wings to row ashore.

B/W illustration Ruth Grewcock

Richard Packwood/Oxford Scientific Films

A pipistrelle devours a caddis fly (above).
A favorite perch often has a litter of
moth wings and other insect
debris beneath it.

Illustration John Cox/Wildlife Art Agency

225

HIBERNATION

All vesper bats roost during the day, retreating to a safe refuge to hang up until the dimming light lures them out to hunt. Most species roost in colonies, but they do not seem to form a complex social structure with elaborate systems of communication; they simply gather in favored sites and often cluster together to keep warm. This heat conservation is crucial for females in the late stages of gestation, for otherwise their bodies would cool down, slowing and even arresting the development of the unborn young.

COLD STORAGE

Unlike us, a bat can safely allow its core body temperature to fluctuate widely, and if it cools down while roosting, its heart rate, breathing, and metabolism slow down, reducing the rate at which it uses stored energy. Naturally it cannot do much while in this condition, but assuming it is not pregnant or nursing young, it hardly needs to.

In temperate latitudes, this capacity for switching into standby mode is a lifesaver. On wet, windy, summer nights the insects often do not fly; there is little point in hunting if there is nothing to

Jose Luis Gonzales Grande/Bruce Coleman Ltd.

A PIPISTRELLE WARMS UP AT THE RATE OF ROUGHLY 1.8°F PER MINUTE, SO IF ITS BODY HAS COOLED BY 18°F IT WILL TAKE 10 MINUTES BEFORE IT IS FIT TO FLY

catch, so the bats stay put and rely on the chilly roost to keep them in cold storage. They can stay in this state for weeks if necessary, but changes in the temperature or disturbances will arouse them.

Waking up is a slow business since the bat has to fire up its internal heating system; as it warms up, its breathing speeds up and it begins to shiver, a mechanism that helps the warming process. This delay makes the bat vulnerable to predators, so a secure roosting site is essential.

HIBERNATION—A LIFESAVER

The onset of winter sweeps most flying insects out of the skies, and a bat that tried to hunt during the northern winter would soon starve. As a flying animal it could theoretically migrate to warmer regions where insects are still abundant, but this would involve a long journey. Swifts, swallows, and flycatchers have to migrate from northern Europe to tropical Africa—but then, they do not have the less strenuous option of hibernating.

(in)SIGHT

BAT MIGRATION

Although vesper bats typically weather the food shortages of winter by hibernating, some species are known to migrate. The North American red bat, for example, may migrate south from Canada to overwinter in Mexico and the West Indies, and the silver-haired bat flies from Canada to Bermuda. The European noctule regularly makes long migrations, and even small bats such as the pipistrelle have been recorded far from their summer roosts.

The reasons for these long journeys are not always clear. Some northern species migrate south in autumn because they prefer hibernating in hollow trees, and the temperatures in such roosts may fall too low in the far north. Yet the red bat, an accomplished migrant, may also stay in the north for the winter: A healthy hibernating red bat was once found with a body temperature of 23°F (-5°C)—the lowest ever recorded for a bat.

SUMMER RETREAT
A bat colony's summer roost site needs to be warm and snug (right), *enabling gestating or nursing females to keep their young in a supportive, stable climate.*

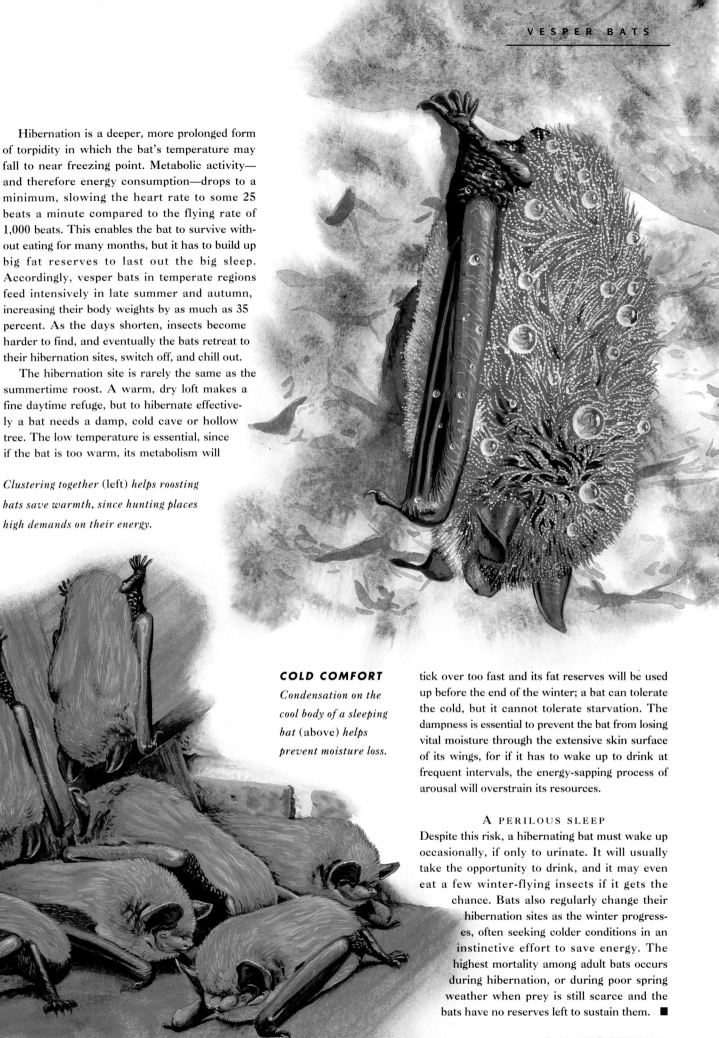

Hibernation is a deeper, more prolonged form of torpidity in which the bat's temperature may fall to near freezing point. Metabolic activity—and therefore energy consumption—drops to a minimum, slowing the heart rate to some 25 beats a minute compared to the flying rate of 1,000 beats. This enables the bat to survive without eating for many months, but it has to build up big fat reserves to last out the big sleep. Accordingly, vesper bats in temperate regions feed intensively in late summer and autumn, increasing their body weights by as much as 35 percent. As the days shorten, insects become harder to find, and eventually the bats retreat to their hibernation sites, switch off, and chill out.

The hibernation site is rarely the same as the summertime roost. A warm, dry loft makes a fine daytime refuge, but to hibernate effectively a bat needs a damp, cold cave or hollow tree. The low temperature is essential, since if the bat is too warm, its metabolism will

Clustering together (left) *helps roosting bats save warmth, since hunting places high demands on their energy.*

COLD COMFORT
Condensation on the cool body of a sleeping bat (above) *helps prevent moisture loss.*

tick over too fast and its fat reserves will be used up before the end of the winter; a bat can tolerate the cold, but it cannot tolerate starvation. The dampness is essential to prevent the bat from losing vital moisture through the extensive skin surface of its wings, for if it has to wake up to drink at frequent intervals, the energy-sapping process of arousal will overstrain its resources.

A PERILOUS SLEEP

Despite this risk, a hibernating bat must wake up occasionally, if only to urinate. It will usually take the opportunity to drink, and it may even eat a few winter-flying insects if it gets the chance. Bats also regularly change their hibernation sites as the winter progresses, often seeking colder conditions in an instinctive effort to save energy. The highest mortality among adult bats occurs during hibernation, or during poor spring weather when prey is still scarce and the bats have no reserves left to sustain them. ■

Illustrations John Cox/Wildlife Art Agency

REPRODUCTION

Among the vesper bats, breeding is governed by the food supply. In the tropics food is abundant all year round, enabling several *Myotis* species to have two or three litters a year. Tropical species that produce single litters can breed whenever it suits them, for there is always prey to sustain the pregnant or lactating females.

In temperate regions it is a different story. Insect prey is scarce in winter and unpredictable at other times. Bats must time the birth of their young carefully to coincide with maximum prey abundance and avoid any serious setbacks that might arise from periods of dormancy. Most northern species are limited to one infant a year, born in late spring when the insects are numerous and the weather is most dependable. In the early stages of pregnancy a shortage of food may force a female to slip into torpor, putting a brake on fetal development; this may be no bad thing, since it ensures that the birth is postponed until better times. But nursing females must keep eating to maintain their milk supply, so once the young are born, a spell of wet, windy weather that keeps the flying insects at home can be a real problem.

ARRESTED DEVELOPMENT

One consequence of this is that although vesper bats typically mate in the autumn, the development of the young in the womb cannot start until early spring, after the female awakes from hibernation. In at least one species—Schreiber's bent-winged bat—the problem is resolved by delayed implantation. This postpones the growth of the fetus by preventing the immediate implantation of the egg in the uterine wall.

Most other vesper bats employ a tactic that is unique to bats. The male's sperm does not instantly fertilize the egg; instead sperm is stored within the female's body for up to seven months. When conditions are right, the female ovulates and conceives. The system ensures that the female is ready to start breeding as soon as she has a dependable food supply, unlike most mammals, which have to go through the mating process first.

MATING

Some vesper bats, such as the Asian painted bat, appear to form monogamous mating pairs, but the males of most species are polygamous. The male bamboo bat of tropical Southeast Asia attracts a harem of females with them year-round, but the males of temperate species typically court as

STAY-AT-HOMES
In most species, the mothers gather in female-only nursery colonies to give birth and rear their young. Ideal nursery sites, with suitably warm and humid conditions, may be reused every year.

MATING
A complex courtship involving singing and flight displays usually precedes copulation (below). *The mating act itself is usually brief, unless it occurs during the hibernation period; if this is the case, the animals may fall asleep in this position.*

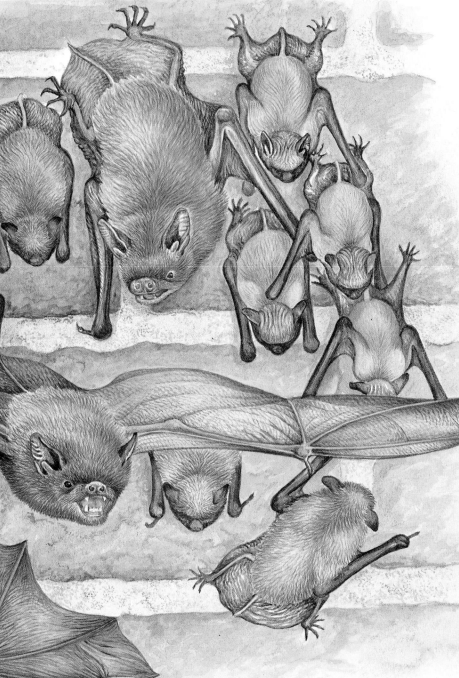

FROM BIRTH TO DEATH

COMMON PIPISTRELLE	BAMBOO BAT
GESTATION: AVERAGE 44 DAYS	**GESTATION:** 90 DAYS
LITTER SIZE: 1, OCCASIONALLY 2	**LITTER SIZE:** USUALLY 2
MATING: AUTUMN	**MATING:** NOVEMBER–FEBRUARY
BIRTH: MIDSPRING	**BIRTH:** FEBRUARY–MAY
WEIGHT AT BIRTH: .04–.07 oz (1–2 G)	**WEIGHT AT BIRTH:** 0.01 oz (0.2 G)
FIRST FLIGHT: 3 WEEKS	**FIRST FLIGHT:** 3 WEEKS
WEANING: 5–6 WEEKS	**WEANING:** 5–6 WEEKS
SEXUAL MATURITY: 1–2 YEARS	**SEXUAL MATURITY:** 1 YEAR
LONGEVITY: UP TO 15 YEARS	**LONGEVITY:** UP TO 15 YEARS

many females as possible in the autumn, mate with them, and then ignore them for the rest of the year. In some species the male uses a favored roost as a base for display flights, calling loudly to lure females. The European noctule attracts up to eighteen females at a time, although he does not keep a harem.

Mating may continue into the hibernation period, but the females do not conceive until spring; indeed, if they enter hibernation in poor condition, they may not conceive at all. The gestation time depends on the spring weather, but in due course the single young is born at the nursery roost, usually dropping into the cupped tail membrane while the mother hangs by her thumbs.

GETTING A GRIP ON LIFE

Naked and blind at birth, the baby can cling to the roost with its claws and, if need be, hitch a ride by gripping its mother's fur with its hooked milk teeth. Usually the mother leaves her infant behind when she hunts, for it would burden her at a time when she needs lots of food. In colonial species, the pink-skinned infants may huddle in crowds on the roof or walls of the roost, with up to 279 per square foot (3,000 per square meter). The crowding helps control their temperature, but it makes identification difficult for mothers when they return to their young; somehow they manage, guided by the infants' scents and squeaks.

After three weeks or so, the young are full-grown and may even fly with the adults, but they suckle for a few weeks longer until they can catch their own food. Bats have an instinctive hunting ability, but it has to be refined by experience; the young adults usually stay with their mothers until the early autumn while they learn the best hunting sites and roost locations. By autumn they will be feeding intensively to prepare for the winter sleep, and their mothers will have mated again. ∎

Gould's long-eared bat is one of the few vesper species to produce twins.

Martis Wildlife Films/Oxford Scientific Films

Illustrations Robin Budden/Wildlife Art Agency

BANISHED FROM HOME

VESPER BATS ARE IN THEIR ELEMENT ON A HOT SUMMER'S NIGHT, WHEN THE STILL AIR IS LADEN WITH PREY. BUT COME WINTER, THEY NEED A QUIET, COOL REFUGE—AND REFUGES ARE INCREASINGLY HARD TO FIND

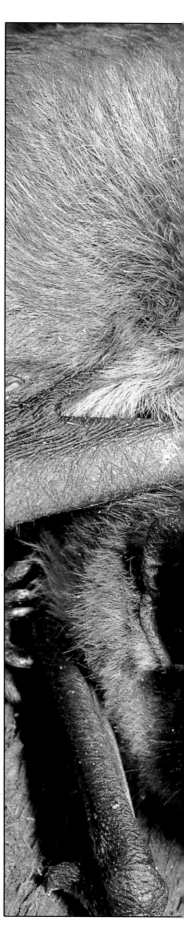

In some parts of the world people eat bats. On the western Pacific island of Guam the local taste for bat meat has led to the annihilation of one species of megachiropteran flying fox—or fruit bat—and the near-extinction of another. The bats are blown out of the sky by hunters armed with shotguns, and the number of bats that are killed instantly and collected for the pot is far outnumbered by the number that die slowly and painfully from infected shotgun wounds.

The vesper bats are not on anyone's menu, but many species are still threatened by human activities. Some suffer direct attack from people who believe that bats are pests and carriers of disease. Others—in fact most vesper bats worldwide—are retreating in the face of habitat erosion as their roost sites are disturbed or destroyed and their rich hunting grounds are swept away in the cause of agriculture, forestry, or urban development. Even the swarms of flying insects that they prey on have dwindled in the face of changing agricultural practice and chemical pest control programs. So although most of us rarely see vesper bats, let alone eat them, we all contribute to their decline.

AGRICULTURAL CHANGES

Modern agricultural methods have created a real problem for insectivorous bats. Traditional mixed farming involved planting a wide range of crops on each farm, rotating them around the fields, and running livestock over the land. In winter stock was fed on hay mown from species-rich meadowland. The variety of plants in the meadows, fields, the hedges between them, the cattle sheds, and dung heaps all encouraged a thriving insect population and therefore plenty of prey for bats, who also enjoyed a wide choice of roosting sites among the farm outbuildings and hedgerow trees.

Recently, however, easy access to artificial fertilizers and chemical pesticides has enabled farmers to plant on the same land year after year. This makes the old rotation systems unnecessary and allows most of the farm to be planted with the most profitable crop. Many farmers have done away with livestock, demolished old outbuildings, and taken out hedgerows to make large fields suitable for big, efficient machines. Devoting such large areas of land to a single crop dramatically reduces the diversity of insect life, and the insects that do thrive often multiply to plague proportions, creating a pest problem that can be controlled only with large amounts of insecticide.

H. Clark/Frank Lane Picture Agency

Bat boxes, with special slit entrances, are in high demand as natural roost sites dwindle (above).

Duncan I. McEwan/Aquila

THEN & NOW

This map shows the approximate current distribution of Leisler's bat, one of Europe's rarer vesper species.

■ **CURRENT DISTRIBUTION**

Leisler's bat is a medium-sized species that lives mainly in forests, particularly where there are plenty of old trees with holes to provide it with roosts. While it is still fairly abundant in Ireland, it is rare over much of the rest of its range in Europe. Like many vesper bats, it is threatened mainly by the deforestation of its favorite habitat. Its close relative, the greater noctule bat, is thought to be one of Europe's rarest bats.

Even farmers who rely on livestock for their profits have adopted systems that reduce the diversity of wild plants and animals. In northern Europe, and particularly in Britain, many dairy farmers have plowed up the old pasture and replaced the mixture of wild grasses with specially bred, highly nutritious varieties such as ryegrass. The traditional practice of hay making to provide winter feed is also giving way to silage making, which involves mowing the grass early and effectively "canning" it to preserve its nutritional value. In combination, these two developments have led to a steep decline in grassland insects such as large beetles, many of which start their lives feeding among the roots of wild grassland plants and complete their life cycles as the plants

Not everybody wants bats in their attic—but it is nevertheless an offense to disturb roosting colonies.

flower, just before the traditional hay cut. Replacing the wild plants with exotic grasses removes the food supply of most of these insects, and cutting the meadows early for silage kills any resident insects before they can disperse and breed.

POISONED PREY

The effect of these farming practices upon bats can be disastrous. The virtual disappearance of many types of insect can effectively wipe out the food supply of some species and dramatically reduce the options available to others. Worse, the use of pesticides does not merely kill insects. As a bat may devour countless insects each night by hunting in a small area, it risks absorbing a damaging or even fatal dose of poison. This risk is particularly serious in the tropics, where organochlorines such as DDT are still widely used to control malarial mosquitoes and similar insect pests. These poisons stay in the environment for many months and build up in the tissues of animals that ingest only tiny quantities at a time. The catastrophic consequences for birds are well known, but we can only guess at their effect on bats.

RUINED ROOSTS

The threat posed by the disappearance and contamination of their prey is compounded by the dwindling number of suitable roosting and hibernation sites, particularly in the densely populated parts of Europe and North America. Old, hollow trees are removed in the cause of good forestry practice, woodlands are bulldozed for agriculture, and broad-leaved forests across the northern

---

RESTING BATS ARE HIGHLY SENSITIVE TO TEMPERATURE FLUCTUATIONS CAUSED BY HUMAN INVASION OF THEIR ROOSTS

---

hemisphere are transformed into conifer plantations for paper production. Conifer plantations not only offer fewer roosting sites; they also support a much-less-varied insect fauna than deciduous woodlands. Picturesque ruins are tidied up for the tourist trade, while less-picturesque ruins are demolished for the benefit of the building trade. Caves are disturbed by spelunkers and, in some parts of the world, by hunters seeking bats for food. Even churches, traditional roosting sites for bats for hundreds of years, are being bat-proofed to calm the nerves of their congregations.

OUR HOME, THEIR HOME

In summer many species will readily roost in the roof spaces of occupied houses, but even if the

Jose Luis Gonzales Grande/Bruce Coleman Ltd.

ENDANGERED ENVIRONMENT

CAVE DANGERS

Cool, moist caves make ideal hibernation sites for many vesper bats, offering stable conditions and plenty of space for roosting. A suitable cave may attract bats from a vast radius and may have done so for thousands of years, to the point of influencing the very evolution of some species. But a cave that was once a safe refuge may be transformed into a tomb.

Inset photograph Wayne Lankinen/Aquila

CONSERVATION MEASURES

● Many known hibernation caves are now protected, and entry is prohibited without special permits. Research on the bats is strictly controlled to minimize disturbance, and most caves are entered only once or twice each winter to monitor bat numbers.

● Bat Conservation International, an organization based in Austin, Texas, has purchased a number of key bat sites to

In Europe and North America the main problem is disturbance by caving enthusiasts. Cave-dwelling bats are very sensitive to the disruption caused by a party of cavers passing through their refuge. Even if the cavers try to keep quiet, the rattle of their equipment, the glare of their lights, and the inevitable changes of scent and temperature will wake up the bats.

Awakening from hibernation is an exhausting process, and by the time the bats are fully alert, they have used up a lot of energy. And as they flutter in alarm around the cave, their energy reserves are drained. Since they have been roused by artificial stimuli rather than, say, good weather, they cannot easily feed to replace the lost energy. It takes very few such intrusions to sap their reserves to the point where they will not survive the winter.

Cave-hibernating species are particularly at risk because suitable caves are scarce; as a result, huge numbers of bats may overwinter in one cave. For example, in the United States some 90 percent of the gray bats living to the south of Kentucky and east of the Mississippi hibernate in just three caves, one of which harbors some 1.5 million bats. Any regular disturbance of just one of these caves would destroy a significant proportion of the species, and disturbances in all three caves could wipe it out altogether.

THE LITTLE BROWN BAT OFTEN ROOSTS IN BARNS AND HOUSES; THESE ARE VULNERABLE HABITATS.

protect them against disturbance, and promotes bat conservation programs the world over.

● The mouths of dangerous caves and disused mines are often blocked to prevent accidents, but in many countries they are now barred with steel grills to ensure that bats can still flit in to gain access to their hibernation sites.

BATS IN DANGER

THE CHART BELOW SHOWS HOW, IN 1994, IUCN CLASSIFIED THE STATUS OF THE VESPER BATS THAT ARE, OR MAY BE, UNDER SERIOUS THREAT:

GRAY BAT	ENDANGERED
INDIANA BAT	VULNERABLE
POND BAT	VULNERABLE
GREATER MOUSE-EARED BAT	VULNERABLE
LONG-FINGERED BAT	VULNERABLE
TOWNSEND'S BIG-EARED BAT	INDETERMINATE
JAVAN THICK-THUMBED BAT	INSUFFICIENTLY KNOWN

ENDANGERED MEANS THAT THE SPECIES IS FACING A HIGH PROBABILITY OF EXTINCTION IN THE NEAR FUTURE. *VULNERABLE* MEANS THAT IT IS LIKELY TO BECOME ENDANGERED IF NOTHING IS DONE TO IMPROVE ITS SITUATION. *INDETERMINATE* MEANS THAT THE SPECIES IS THREATENED AND MAY POSSIBLY BE ENDANGERED. *INSUFFICIENTLY KNOWN* MEANS THAT THE SPECIES IS PROBABLY THREATENED, BUT MORE PRECISE INFORMATION IS LACKING.

householder does not deliberately evict them, they are at risk from more insidious threats. Of these, the most serious is the chemical treatment of roof timbers for woodworm and deathwatch beetle. The chemicals employed are often powerful, long-lasting poisons, and while they make short work of insect pests, they are equally lethal to bats. Any bats who even investigate a freshly treated roof space may be dead within a day or two, and some ill effects may be suffered by bats taking up residence years after the treatment.

Another problem is cavity-wall insulation—the injection of foamed plastic insulating material into the cavities between the double-skinned outer brick walls of modern houses. Such cavities can provide cool, moist hibernation sites for small bats, but pumping the gap full of foam denies them the option. If there are bats in residence when the work is done, they may be poisoned or trapped. Other measures designed to make houses more weatherproof or easier to maintain can have similar consequences: Ripping off clapboards and replacing them with plastic sheeting, for example, can destroy a good roosting site.

FEAR AND IGNORANCE

Many householders who undertake such work are not aware that they are disturbing a bat roost. Bats are elusive creatures that may come and go for years quite unobserved by the humans that share their habitat. But when they congregate in large numbers, their presence becomes obvious,

ALONGSIDE MAN

BATS IN THE ATTIC

The roof spaces of occupied houses are vital roosting sites for many bats, particularly smaller species, such as the European common pipistrelle, which can slip through narrow gaps and roost comfortably in surprisingly small spaces. A colony of 100 pipistrelles could easily roost in the woodwork at the gable end of a roof, and colonies of 500 or more are not uncommon. More usually the bats congregate in smaller groups, and since they lie low in daylight, the only evidence of their presence is their droppings. These are dark, dry, and quite innocuous, being composed mainly of indigestible insect fragments such as beetle wing cases. As many of these may be the remains of insect pests—including furniture beetles (woodworms) and other timber destroyers—there are good practical reasons for welcoming any bats that take up residence, and many householders find the interest value alone sufficient reward. If the resident bats are a nuisance for some reason, the nearest wildlife-conservation authority will alert the local bat experts to the problem, and they will advise on the best course of action—bearing in mind that bats are now strictly protected by law in many countries.

and some people find the idea of bats living under the same roof extremely unpleasant. Bats inspire fear in many people, partly because of the way they flit about in the dark, but mostly because of the myths that surround them. They are associated with vampires, ghosts, and graveyards. Their leathery wings are among the traditional attributes of the devil. For some reason they are believed to have an irresistible attraction for human hair, taking every opportunity to become ensnared in it. More understandably, it is assumed that they are dirty, that they carry disease, and that their droppings are a health hazard.

CHANGING OPINION

These attitudes have led to the pointless destruction of countless bat roosts. In the United States a fear of bats has been deliberately promoted to drum up business for the pest-control industry, which encourages people to classify bats as vermin. In the United Kingdom and Europe the common fear of bats is now being tempered by a growing awareness that these fears are groundless—an awareness largely brought about by wildlife films on television—and today a colony of bats in the roof space is often regarded with interest and even pride. In any case, such colonies are now protected by law throughout Europe and many other countries, and householders with resident bats are legally obliged to keep disturbance

to a minimum and carry out essential repair work only after consulting the conservation authorities.

Such legislation, and the shifts in public opinion that inspired it, has certainly prevented a lot of destruction in recent years, yet for many vesper bats these measures have come too late. The environment has already changed too radically, and the resulting loss of food resources and roosting sites means that they will never fully recover.

To some extent, expanding human settlement has helped sustain many bat colonies by providing roosting sites in churches and outbuildings. With this in mind, developers who modernize farmland or dwellings may claim some justification in taking away from bats what was freely given them in the first place. Against this argument, however, stands the fact that the wholesale felling of ancient woodlands did away with much of the bats' original habitat. Today, whether we like it or not, we are the guardians of a high proportion of bat populations. And their continued decline in the future is something we can still prevent. ∎

In central Europe, populations of the greater mouse-eared bat have fallen by some 80 percent.

M. Andera/Natural Science Photos

INTO THE FUTURE

Illustration Kim Thompson

Throughout the world bats are in decline, and several species have recently died out. The vesper bats have fared better than some, however, and only nine of the 319 known species were listed as under threat or extinct by the IUCN Species Survival Commission in 1994. This may be because vesper bats, being relatively unspecialized, are better able to exploit altered environments; certainly some species, such as the North American big brown bat—originally a forest dweller—have successfully adapted to urban life.

Major changes to European farmland occurred in the 1970s and 1980s, when arable farming was highly subsidized under the European Community's Common Agricultural Policy, encouraging the "reclamation" of old grasslands, wetlands, and scrub for agriculture. This policy has since lapsed, and farmers are now

---

PREDICTION

ADAPTABLE AND RESILIENT

Some North American species, such as the gray and Indiana bats, are at risk owing to a scarcity of roosting sites. On the whole, however, vespers are highly successful bats with a proven ability to adapt to, and survive in, an ever-changing world.

---

encouraged to allow less productive land to revert to nature. Financial grants are also given for planting deciduous woodlands and conserving existing woodland, wetland, and ancient grassland. If this continues, the habitats of many vesper bats will stop shrinking and may even expand.

Elsewhere in the world, where land use is less intensive, bats are generally more abundant, but their outlook is possibly bleaker. As developing countries continue to exploit their resources many habitats will be destroyed; several tropical species are already threatened by deforestation. Their food supplies are also more likely to be contaminated by pesticides: DDT is still widely used in the tropics, and, although it is banned in the United States, many North American species are affected by DDT use in Mexico. So while the worst is possibly over for vesper bats in the developed world, where wildlife is becoming an affordable luxury, their relatives in cash-starved countries may soon be in serious trouble. ■

BATS AND THE LAW

In the United States selected species are federally listed as threatened or endangered, and each state has its own laws. However, the provisions of the United Kingdom Wildlife and Countryside Act of 1981 typify most European legislation and cover three main aspects of conservation.

● Direct attacks on bats are illegal. Bats are not harmful, and there is no reason to injure one. Unnecessary handling is also illegal, but you are permitted to remove a bat from your living space (the rooms in the house) or tend an injured bat.

● Damaging a roosting or hibernation site, or obstructing its entrance, is illegal. Since the entrances to these may be gaps in brickwork or timber that need repair, many householders break the law simply by maintaining their property. If bats are present, contact the local wildlife authority for advice.

● Disturbing bats at roost is illegal. This applies to hibernation sites in caves, old mine workings, and hollow trees, and also to summer roosts in buildings, where the bats may raise their young.

BAT BOXES

In areas where natural roosting sites are scarce, bats can benefit from artificial roosting boxes. These are like bird boxes but have a slot in the base instead of a hole on the front. Bat boxes are easy to make using unsanded, untreated wood. A bat box needs to be mounted high up, preferably on a tree trunk and facing south or west if possible. Bats are suspicious of new premises, however, and a box may stay empty for years before being used. Even then the bats may not stay long, but since up to 40 bats may squeeze into one box, this hardly matters.

AMERICAN BLACK BEARS

RELATIONS

Bears belong to the order Carnivora and the family Ursidae. Other members of the family include:

BROWN BEARS

POLAR BEAR

ASIAN BLACK BEAR

Daniel J. Cox/Oxford Scientific Films

CLASSIFICATION

Along with all other bears, the American black bear is classed as a carnivore. Most of the mammals in the group are predominantly flesh eating, but in common with a few others, bears have an infinitely more varied diet. The order Carnivora includes cats, dogs, raccoons, pandas, weasels, badgers, skunks, otters, civets, mongooses, and hyenas.

ORDER

Carnivora
(carnivores)

FAMILY

Ursidae
(bears)

GENUS

Ursus

SPECIES

americanus

BLACK AND BLUE BRUISERS

ALTHOUGH ALWAYS KNOWN AS THE BLACK BEAR, THIS UNIQUELY NORTH AMERICAN BEAR MAY ACTUALLY SPORT A COAT OF A VARIETY OF COLORS FROM ALMOST WHITE, THROUGH BLUE-BLACK, TO COAL-BLACK

Unperturbed by the visitors' cars in the clearing of a forest in Yellowstone National Park, United States, a stocky figure emerges from the woods and ambles over to the rubbish bins. Rearing on its hind legs, it thrusts its head deep into the bin and starts rifling through the contents. A black bear has set out in search of an easy meal. If its hunger is not satisfied, it may pace around the cars, stopping occasionally by the side of one to sit back on its haunches and wave its forepaws in the air—begging for food from the people inside.

Smaller than America's other well-known bear, the brown or grizzly bear, the American black bear has proved itself infinitely adaptable to the trappings of humankind that have invaded its world. Its natural curiosity, and nearly insatiable hunger, soon led it to realize that civilization brought benefits such as abundant food, as careless visitors would leave picnic boxes within reach.

A sapling provides a convenient back scratcher for this yearling (right).

Long since a symbol of North America's one-time wild and uninhabited tracts of rocky, wooded country, the bears' ancestors probably made their first appearance on Earth in North America during the Miocene epoch, which spanned from 25 to 5 million years ago. It was, in fact, not until 5 or 6 million years ago that bears became more abundant

ONE OF THE BLACK BEAR'S LONG-EXTINCT RELATIVES WAS THE CAVE BEAR, A CONTEMPORARY OF EARLY HUMANS

and widespread. Numbers of bears evolved—some of them very large—and died out. The genus *Ursus*, to which six of today's bears belong, appeared around 3 million years ago.

The American black bear was given its name by North America's early settlers because of the color of its coat, but this can be misleading. The so-called black bear may have a coat of almost blue, gray, a cinnamon brown, beige, or, perhaps most dramatic of all, a creamy white. These color variations generally occur within different locations.

Daniel J. Cox/Oxford Scientific Films

Erwin & Peggy Baeur/Bruce Coleman Ltd.

A bear with food on its mind has no greater asset than its moist, superbly sensitive nose (above).

THE SHUFFLING BEAR

Daniel J. Cox/Oxford Scientific Films

Like all bears, the American black bear walks in a plantigrade manner—that is, on the heels, then soles of its feet, in the same way that a human does. Usually it moves around on all fours in a clumsy, shuffling walk, its forefeet turned inward in a pigeon-toed fashion. When tracks are visible on the ground, such as in soft earth or mud, the front and hind tracks are paired, with the hind tracks placed in front of the front tracks on the same side. The stride is usually about 12 in (30 cm) long.

Although it moves slowly in its daily life, the American black bear can move impressively fast if it needs to: up to 30 mph (48 km/h). It achieves this in a kind of bounding trot or gallop in which the hind feet hit the ground well in front of the forefeet, and the stride may reach 36 in (90 cm) or more.

The creamy white bear, often known as the Kermode bear, is found only in a few isolated areas of British Columbia. Sometimes the coat is deeper in color, ranging through a yellow or orangy hue to almost chestnut. The blue bear, or glacier bear, occurs in the mountains of southeastern Alaska, but in its pure blue form is now thought to be very rare.

All bears share a basic, recognizable shape: a bulky body, a fairly big head with small, rounded ears, stocky, powerful limbs, and a short tail. The American black bear is considerably smaller than its brown bear relatives, even though its size varies widely depending on its location. Those in the eastern sections of the range can weigh up to twice as much as those in the west.

The American black bear has a longer, more pointed muzzle than the grizzly bear, and its facial profile is less concave. Its ears are larger in proportion to its face. It also generally lacks the shoulder hump of many grizzlies, although if it stands in a certain position, it can appear to possess this. It has shorter hind feet and the claws are inconspicuous, whereas they are very prominent in the grizzly. Whatever the color of the fur, the muzzle is usually chestnut colored. The fur is shorter than that of the grizzly bear, but even so it tends to make the bear look deceptively large.

THE FORWARD-FACING EYES ARE TYPICAL OF CARNIVORES—ALTHOUGH, IN FACT, THE BLACK BEAR IS MAINLY VEGETARIAN

As with all bears, smell is the most highly developed sense. The nose is permanently wet, and the American black bear often sits up on its haunches, sniffing the air in a doglike manner for clues about its surroundings. Bears are generally credited with poor vision; it certainly is not as acute as in many carnivores, but they can spot movement at quite long distances.

The American black bear is generally silent, although it does have a few vocalizations. It barks when startled, and emits a low, menacing growl if forced into confrontation with another bear. Cubs howl shrilly to attract their mother when distressed. Unlike the grizzly, the American black bear takes readily to the trees, climbing fairly frequently—and expertly—either to escape from humans or grizzlies or to search for food. It is also a powerful swimmer with no fear of water.   ∎

ANCESTORS

The ancestors of today's carnivores were a family of small, tree-climbing mammals known as the miacids, which are thought to have given rise to coyotes, wolves, foxes, raccoons, and dogs. Bears evolved from the early dog family, their first representative being a small animal known as the dawn bear, *Ursus elemensis*.

The early true bears evolved in Europe, but representatives probably crossed the Bering land bridge that linked North America to northeastern Asia, one or two million years ago. The most common bear of the time was a large but slight-framed animal known as the short-faced bear.

BROWN BEAR
Ursus arctos
(*UR-sus ARK-tos*)

ASIAN BLACK BEAR
Ursus thibetanus
(*UR-sus tib-et-AHN-us*)

B/W illustrations Ruth Grewcock

SPECTACLED BEAR
Tremarctos ornatus
(*trem-ARK-tos or-NAH-tus*)

THE AMERICAN BLACK BEAR'S FAMILY TREE

Contained within the bear family, Ursidae, are the world's largest land-living carnivores: the grizzly bear and the polar bear. These two bears, also found in North America, belong to the same genus, Ursus, as the American black bear, the Asian black bear, the sun bear, and the sloth bear. The spectacled bear and the giant panda are each placed in a separate genus, of which they are the only members. The giant panda has only recently been recognized as a bear.

POLAR BEAR
Ursus maritimus
(UR-sus marri-TEE-mus)

BEST KNOWN SUBSPECIES:
KERMODE BEAR
BLUE OR GLACIER
    BEAR
CINNAMON BEAR
EASTERN BLACK
    BEAR
NEWFOUNDLAND
    BLACK BEAR
EVERGLADES
    BEAR

AMERICAN BLACK BEAR
Ursus americanus (UR-sus ah-merri-CAHN-us)

Possessing features and characteristics typical of most bears, the American black bear is the smallest of the three bears found in North America. Up to 18 different subspecies are recognized, identifiable from each other by their coat color, location, and, to some extent, size.

SUN BEAR
Ursus malayanus
(UR-sus mah-lay-AHN-us)

SLOTH BEAR
Ursus ursinus
(UR-sus ur-SEE-nus)

DAWN BEAR

Color illustrations Steve Kingston

241

ANATOMY:
THE BLACK BEAR

The American black bear varies in size but has a maximum head-and-body length of 6 ft (183 cm) and shoulder height of 3 ft (91 cm). That is much smaller than the polar bear, which may be up to 8 ft (243 cm) in length with a shoulder height of 5 ft (152 cm).

Anatomy illustrations Wayne Ford/Wildlife Art Agency

FOREFOOT

HIND FOOT

THE NOSE

is black and wet, giving an acute sense of smell. All bears sit back on their haunches and sniff the air. The muzzle is generally brown.

THE FEET

all have five toes, with the largest toe outermost. The claws are usually about 2.5 in (6.3 cm) long. The hind feet are more heavily padded than the forefeet.

TRACKS

typically show the heavily padded hind foot set in front of the forefoot.

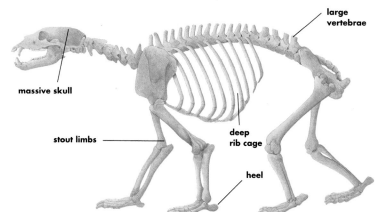

BLACK BEAR SKELETON

The skeleton is characterized by a heavy bone structure. The spine is short and almost horizontal in profile. The rib cage is deep and barrel shaped. The bones of the feet are long, with pronounced heels, reflecting the bear's plantigrade (flat-footed) method of walking.

large vertebrae

massive skull

stout limbs

deep rib cage

heel

SKULL (RIGHT)

The big head of all bears comprises a skull that is the longest, with the most massive bone structure, of all carnivores. With plenty of bone to anchor on, powerful jaw muscles give a formidable bite.

X-ray illustrations Elisabeth Smith

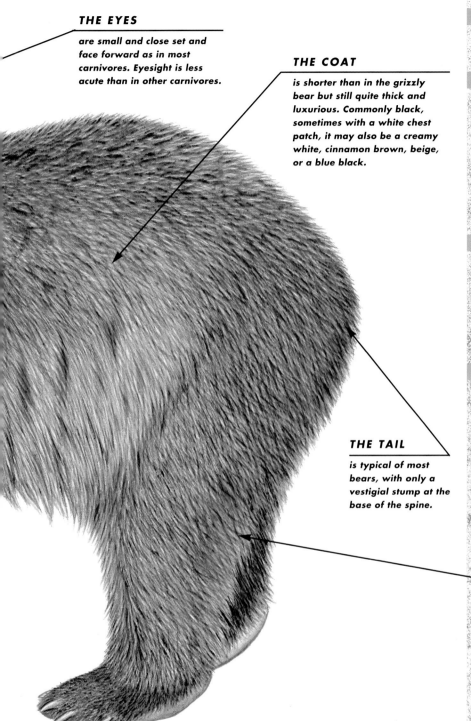

THE EYES

are small and close set and face forward as in most carnivores. Eyesight is less acute than in other carnivores.

THE COAT

is shorter than in the grizzly bear but still quite thick and luxurious. Commonly black, sometimes with a white chest patch, it may also be a creamy white, cinnamon brown, beige, or a blue black.

THE TAIL

is typical of most bears, with only a vestigial stump at the base of the spine.

AMERICAN BLACK BEAR

CLASSIFICATION

GENUS: *URSUS*

SPECIES: *AMERICANUS*

SIZE

HEAD–BODY LENGTH: 5–6 FT (152–183 CM)

SHOULDER HEIGHT: 3 FT (91 CM)

TAIL LENGTH: 5 IN (12.7 CM)

WEIGHT/MALE: 250–600 LB (113–272 KG)

WEIGHT AT BIRTH: 8–12 OZ (248–373 G)

THE ADULT MALE IS 10–50 PERCENT HEAVIER THAN THE FEMALE

COLORATION

COMMONLY JET-BLACK, OCCASIONALLY WITH A WHITE CHEST PATCH, BUT COAT COLOR MAY VARY FROM CREAMY WHITE, CINNAMON BROWN, AND BEIGE TO BLACK, OR BLACK WITH A PRONOUNCED BLUE SHEEN. MUZZLE IS USUALLY BROWN.

FEATURES

IN COMPARISON WITH THE GRIZZLY BEAR, THE FRAME IS SMALLER, THE COAT SHORTER, THE FACE MORE CONVEX IN PROFILE, THE MUZZLE MORE POINTED, THE EARS LARGER IN PROPORTION, THE BACK LESS SLOPING, AND THE CLAWS SHORTER.

THE LIMBS

are short and stocky but immensely powerful, enabling the bear to run at speed and also to deliver crushing blows to enemies.

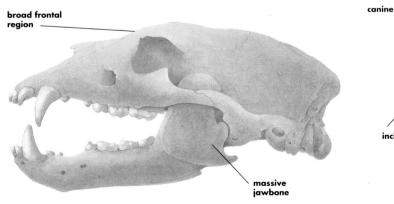

broad frontal region

massive jawbone

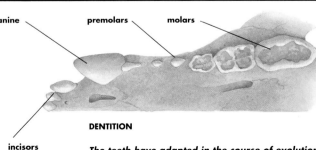

canine

premolars

molars

incisors

DENTITION

The teeth have adapted in the course of evolution to suit a more plant-based diet. The incisors are not specialized for tearing at flesh, the canines are short and strong, and the molars are broad and flat with rounded cusps—ideal for grinding plant material. The teeth grow slowly throughout the bear's life.

LONE RANGER

SOLITARY BY NATURE, LIKE MOST BEARS, THE AMERICAN BLACK BEAR MAY NEVERTHELESS BE SEEN IN THE COMPANY OF OTHERS WHENEVER AND WHEREVER THERE IS AN EASY AND PLENTIFUL FOOD SUPPLY

The American black bear is primarily nocturnal, although it may be seen at almost any time of day or night. Increasingly it wanders in the national parks in daylight hours, for it has learned that tourist cars generally mean easy meals. It is not unusual to find a number of American black bears congregating around rubbish dumps, scavenging through the rubbish for anything edible.

The most numerous and widespread of North America's bears, it leaves evidence of its presence that is easy to recognize. Trees are often scarred with tooth marks that may extend as high up the trunk as the bear can reach standing on its hind legs. Sometimes the bark is stripped (see page 258). The bear also uses tree trunks as scratching posts, and long claw marks—usually diagonal, but sometimes vertical or horizontal—are a common sight in

TENSION IS HIGH IN THE MATING SEASON, WHEN RICH FEEDING SITES LURE JOSTLING NUMBERS OF HIGHLY SEXED MALE BEARS

bear country. In the springtime, clumps of hair may be found snagged on the trunks of rough-barked trees; newly emerged from a winter sleep, the black bear will rub against a trunk to rid itself of loose hair and irritating itches.

With a large hunger to satisfy, an American black bear leaves many clues as to where—and on what—it has been feeding. Logs and stones may be overturned to reveal freshly exposed ground, soil may be scratched up, underground burrows excavated, and anthills torn open. Bushes sporting a good crop of berries will bear evidence of extensive plunder, and branches on fruit trees may have been broken. Feces expelled at random are similar to those of a dog: usually dark brown and coiled, often

with evidence of animal hair, fruit seeds, shells of nuts, and indigestible parts of insects. When a bear has been feasting on berries, the feces tend to be more liquid and very dark in color.

Their solitary nature means that American black bears tend to avoid picking fights with one another. If a number have gathered at a food source, apart from a few rumbling growls, they tend to respect a definite pecking order. Should an encounter occur, it usually begins with the animals "jawing." Facing its adversary, often still in a sitting position, each bear nods its head back and forth with the mouth open, while growling softly. One or the other usually retreats at this point, but if neither does, they then face each other on all fours with forelegs stiffened, heads held low, and ears pressed back, with their mouths opened more widely to bare the canines. They may then charge at one another, but ultimately the weaker one will back away, with its mouth shut and the head facing away.

A yearling marks out his newly established territory on an aspen tree (right).

A black bear investigates the mound of a beaver lodge in Wyoming (above).

Jonathan T. Wright/Bruce Coleman Ltd.

Daniel J. Cox/Oxford Scientific Films

Tussles between bears usually occur during the mating season, when males compete over females.

Mark Newman/Frank Lane Picture Agency

A solitary nature leaves little reason for communication, and bears rarely use facial expressions to show moods—except perhaps by showing the whites of their eyes when angry. The subtle pose of ears and jaws, as well as some body postures, are the best clues to a bear's possible reaction. The ears, for example, project straight forward during a normal, relaxed mood, but the bear can press them back to signify aggression and will prick them up and out when something has caught its attention.

Tree-climbing is a legacy inherited in bears from their first ancestors, the miacids. In today's bears, it occurs to a greater or lesser degree according to the species—the heavier grizzly, for example, rarely

FOLKLORE RELATES THAT A BLACK BEAR WILL CLIMB A TREE TO FIND FOOD, WHILE A GRIZZLY WILL SIMPLY UPROOT IT

climbs. The American black bear, on the other hand, is an agile and frequent climber, as often as not in order to escape from a pursuing grizzly, which is one of its few enemies in the wild.

During a leisurely climb—to raid a bees' nest, for example—the bear takes a few running steps toward the trunk and makes two or three hops up the tree. Then it wraps its forelegs round the trunk, hugging it tightly, and "walks" up as high as it wants to go. But when fleeing from danger, it continues to hop up the trunk, using its forelegs and claws to hang on and balance itself. When descending the tree, the bear always goes backward. ■

245

HABITATS

Like all animals in the wild, the American black bear chooses its habitat to provide all the factors it needs for its daily life—places where food abounds, at least in easily reached areas, and where there are numbers of drinking spots and others for resting, sleeping, and denning (see page 252). Right across its extensive range, the American black bear finds these factors most to its liking in woodland habitats, and it is essentially a

IN SOME AREAS THE BLACK BEAR BENEFITS FROM BEING AN EXCELLENT TOURIST ATTRACTION

forest dweller. In eastern parts it will be found mainly in wooded areas and swamps, while in the west it seeks forests and wooded mountains, although it seldom ventures higher than 7,000 ft (2,100 m). Hardwood forests or the vast coniferous plantations are equally acceptable, and if there are intermittent open areas, which tend to give a greater variety of food, so much the better.

The American black bear's woodland is essentially the temperate rain forests of America, where the characteristic climate is wet and mild and many of the trees grow very tall. A prime example is the Olympic rain forest on the western Olympic Peninsula, in Washington State. Here

DISTRIBUTION

The American black bear occurs mainly in Canada and the northern United States, with a more scattered distribution farther south (see Then & Now, page 289).

KEY

AMERICAN BLACK BEAR

COLOR VERSUS HABITAT

Research done into the varying coat colors of American black bears has led some scientists to believe that the variations may have a link to the type of climate and conditions within an area. Studies conducted on bears foraging over the south-facing slopes of parts of Montana's Rocky Mountains, soon after emerging from the winter's denning, revealed that brown and light-colored bears were able to stay out on the slopes, as the midday sun became ever hotter, longer than the bears with black coats. In an area of Washington State that is characterized by cool, moist forests, black-coated bears predominated while less than 100 mi (160 km) away, in a markedly drier area, nearly 60 percent of the bears were apparently brown.

Daniel J. Cox/Oxford Scientific Films

Zefa

KEY FACTS

● When describing an American black bear they have seen, most people overestimate the size by at least a factor of two, largely because the heavy fur makes it look bigger.

● Carnivores that are not purely flesh eating, such as the bear, are usually considerably slower moving than those that hunt live animals as the main part of their diet.

● A bear's flat-footed stance makes it easy for the animal to stand up on its hind legs. It can even shuffle along for a few paces in this position—a movement developed in the "dancing bears" of street entertainers and circuses.

A black bear crossing a river on a fallen log (left) *in the dense forests of Washington State, United States.*

A cub finds another use for a log—as a crude but effective form of river transport (below).

on the western U.S. coast, the rain clouds from the Pacific Ocean discharge their heavy load to produce lush, abundant plant growth. The temperature never drops below freezing in winter, and the forest streams are well stocked with fish to supplement the bear's diet. The forest floor provides a rich hunting ground as debris collects in the form of leaf litter, dead twigs and branches, fallen rotting tree trunks, and considerable vegetation. This area is often so densely overgrown that progress through it can be difficult for a large animal such as a bear, which is why it tends to have established regular paths and tracks.

The range of the American black bear extends from the northern tree limit of the Arctic, south through most of Canada, Alaska, and Central America, down to the wooded Sierra Madre Mountains into northern Mexico. The bear still

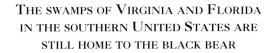

THE SWAMPS OF VIRGINIA AND FLORIDA IN THE SOUTHERN UNITED STATES ARE STILL HOME TO THE BLACK BEAR

exists in more than twenty states and in all Canadian territories and provinces. It was once more widespread, before humans reduced its forest habitat. Generally it is more widespread in the wild in the north of its range; in the south and east it is scattered or else confined to national parks.

TERRITORIES

Each bear will wander over a recognized territory within its range, although these can vary dramatically in size. The territory of a lone female, or a mother with her young, has been known to vary from 1–36 sq miles (2.5–94 sq km). Males may wander over an even larger area—up to five times larger than that of a female. Although it does not generally defend its territory fiercely or even mark it out as other animals do, a male usually keeps to his own area and does not overlap with any other males. A female's range may overlap with that of one or more males and occasionally of other females. In instances of overlap, each bear seems to retain a small core area that is its own exclusive domain. During the mating season, females defend their territories more deliberately. It seems that, in areas below a cutoff point (which varies in size according to location), breeding is less successful.

Within its home range, the American black bear travels along well-worn trails; indeed, trails have often been used by generations of bears that have inhabited the same territory. Generally the bear avoids open areas, keeping to the woodland interior, or at least the edge where there is still some cover. Sometimes it uses stream beds as paths, probably because these creeks also provide shelter from the elements and cover from intruders.

Some zoologists believe that the claw marks found on trees, if not actually boundary or territorial markings, could be made by a male bear to warn off other males as the breeding season approaches. Apparently such markings are more abundant in the weeks before mating occurs.

William M. Smithey Jr./Planet Earth Pictures

FOCUS ON

THE ROCKY MOUNTAINS

The Rocky Mountains stretch the whole length of North America, from Alaska, down through Canada, south through the western United States to the Mexican border. The entire length is some 3,000 mi (4,800 km), and in places they are 400 mi (645 km) wide. The overall elevations vary in height from a mere 985 ft (300 m) to an imposing 14,450 ft (4,399 m). The highest mountain, Mount McKinley, is actually 20,300 ft (6,194 m); it is situated in Alaska.

Within the different elevations, the terrain and vegetation vary considerably. In many northern regions snow-capped peaks dominate the scenery and the tree line is considerably lower than it is farther south in the more temperate areas. Forests below the snow line are usually dominated by coniferous trees—pine, spruce, and fir—but at lower levels there are woods of beech, birch, and the wild fruit trees beloved by the American black bear. Inevitably such a mixed terrain attracts a huge variety of wildlife; within the range, among other mammals, there are wolves, pronghorns, coyotes, wolverines, and elk, as well as bears and numerous small rodents.

Within the length of the Rocky Mountains a number of national parks have been established, among them the Rocky Mountain National Park in north-central Colorado and the Glacier Bay National Park that crosses the border between southern Canada and the northern United States. Both are home to the American black bear.

TEMPERATURE AND RAINFALL

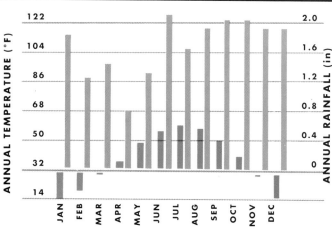

- TEMPERATURE
- RAINFALL

The climate figures for Prince George, in Canada's Rocky Mountains, tell of a cold, damp region. Snowfall is heavy through much of the winter, with temperatures remaining low even in the height of summer.

In the northern and northwestern parts of its range, the American black bear shares its habitats with the much larger grizzly bear. The fact that the two occasionally compete for food probably explains in part why the American black bear tends to be smaller in the Northwest than it does in eastern parts. A grizzly bear will quite often attack a black bear, and its stronger limbs and longer claws pack a deadly punch. One account tells of a grizzly sending a black bear flying over 16 ft (4.8 m) backward into a tree with a single blow from a forepaw, killing it instantly. ∎

NEIGHBORS

The huge variety in climate, vegetation, and terrain along the length of the Rocky Mountains in Canada gives rise to a vast array of wildlife.

TIMBER WOLF

The timber or gray wolf lives in packs and roams widely through the tundra and forests of the north.

MARMOT

This native of woods and pastures on the lower slopes is known also as the woodchuck or groundhog.

Illustrations Kim Thompson

THE ROCKIES

From Alaska in the north, the Rockies follow the western U.S./Canadian seaboard as far as Vancouver, south of which they are found farther inland, in Montana, Wyoming, and Colorado. The montane ridge continues into Mexico in the form of the Sierra Madre.

▨ THE ROCKY MOUNTAINS

VANCOUVER · CALGARY

UNITED STATES

Inset picture Jeff Foote/Survival Anglia

BIGHORN SHEEP	LYNX	ELK	MULE DEER	BLUEBIRD

This hardy, footsure wild sheep favors the foothills and alpine meadows near rocky cliffs.

This wildcat of the deep forests in the northern Rockies has sensitive ear tufts to help it track prey.

In winter, the elk moves from the high mountain pastures to the sheltered lower wooded slopes.

This pretty, large-eared deer lives in many different habitats along almost the entire length of the Rockies.

The male of this bird has a pure sky-blue back, with a paler belly. The female is a little duller.

FOOD AND FEEDING

Undoubtedly, the fact that the American black bear eats such a huge variety of food, and really will test just about anything to see if it is edible, is the key to its continued success as a species.

The black bear's daily food requirement averages around 15 lb (7 kg). Although it is classed as a carnivore, at least 75 percent of its food comes from vegetation. Depending on the season and the availability, it feeds off grass, herbs, twigs, leaves, and young shoots of trees and shrubs as well as newly sprouted plants, corn, acorns and beechnuts, roots, tubers, bulbs and berries, and fruits of all sorts—wild cherries are a particular favorite. It supplements this with insects and grubs that it scratches from rotting logs, under stones or from the soil. It plunders honeycomb, bees, and their larvae from wild bees' nests, which it rips open with its claws. It hunts down and kills small to medium-sized mammals, some of which it digs from their burrows. Moose calves in Alaska often fall prey to the black bear, as do lemmings in northern Canada, although

---

THE BLACK BEAR HAS BEEN DESCRIBED AS A "FOUR-LEGGED GARBAGE GRINDER" THAT EATS "ANYTHING AND EVERYTHIING"

---

these often prove too quick to catch. If the bear finds ground-nesting birds and their eggs in the undergrowth, it will devour them. It is said, too, to have a liking for porcupines, flipping them over deftly with a paw and attacking the soft underbelly. Bears have been spotted sweeping mountain goats off ledges and dragging beavers from lakes.

Being an able swimmer, the black bear often fishes in streams, lakes, or shallow rivers, particularly for salmon, which is also a favorite among brown bears (see Fishing Bears, page 251). In coastal areas it may also eat marine invertebrates and consume animal carcasses or dead fish washed up on beaches or the shores of a lake.

In the coastal timber districts of northern California, Oregon, Washington, and southern British Columbia, the American black bear has come into serious conflict with foresters as it strips the bark of trees such as the Douglas fir to get to the inner juicy layers of cambium. A single bear can rip into some 50 trees in one night, causing more than $20,000 damage in one springtime.

The black bear's "try-anything" diet has also brought it into conflict with humans through its behavior in the national parks. It is the only North American bear to have adapted to human civilization, probably because it has quickly learned that where there are people, there is also food. Besides raiding rubbish dumps and garbage cans, the bear

Color illustrations Guy Troughton/Wildlife Art Agency

INSECTS

BERRIES

YOUNG DEER

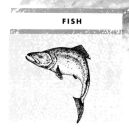

YOUNG BIRDS & EGGS

FISH

B/W illustrations Ruth Grewcock

FEEDING

Black bears are truly omnivorous, taking whatever comes most easily within their range. They readily kill and consume prey such as small mammals, as well as browse on berries and snatch fish from forest streams.

in SIGHT

FISHING BEARS

Although young cubs will often wait nervously on the banks of streams while their mothers fish, it seems unlikely they are learning her technique, for each bear seems to adopt its own unique way of fishing. Some stand very close to the bank, watching the water intently, then suddenly reaching under the surface with a paw and flipping a fish out onto the bank. Others prefer to wade farther into the river, perhaps even swimming to a rock in deeper water and using this as a vantage point. Now the technique is to dive into the water and pin a fish to the riverbed with a paw, breaking its back. Whichever the method, the bear takes its catch to dry land to eat it. It pulls off the flesh from one side with its teeth, eats it, then neatly turns the fish over to pick the other side clean. It often discards the head, tail, and bones.

happily smashes into cabins and wrecks campsites in search of pickings. In many of the national parks, visitors have returned to cars after a few hours' hike only to find them broken open. Broken windows are commonplace, and some bears have even managed to rip off car doors.

The bear's teeth are evidence of its broad diet. Although its canines are long, usually associated with piercing flesh during a kill, the carnassials, or flesh-tearing teeth, are not developed. The cheek teeth, or molars, are adapted for crushing the masses of vegetable matter in the bear's meals.

THE BEAR USES ITS PAWS TO TURN OVER STONES, TRAP FISH AND KILL MAMMALS, AND GATHER BERRIES AND FRUITS

The American black bear spends most of its active time foraging for food. Generally it stays within a fairly small area for days on end, moving on as seasonal foods become available elsewhere. Rarely a frenzied feeder, the bear simply wanders around its territory, turning over stones, investigating rotten logs and tree trunks, digging up roots, insects, and small mammals, and pulling at tasty vegetation. Quite often it sits back on its haunches to feed on a shrub, then merely shuffles on to the next one without changing position. ■

DENNING

Illustration Evi Antoniou

W hen it is not feeding, the American black bear spends its time resting or sleeping, usually in a well-sheltered lair. It may also sleep in the fork of a tree branch, safe from marauding grizzlies.

The black bear often constructs a daytime bed, mainly for resting after a heavy meal. This is usually in a thicket close to good feeding grounds. The bear may dig out a shallow scrape, or simply trample the vegetation to make a cozy hollow.

In most parts of its range, as autumn draws on, the bear begins to feed in a more frenzied manner: It may gain 30 lb (14 kg) in a week at this time. It does this to lay down fat reserves that will last it through the winter, for most black bears spend the cold months asleep in specially prepared dens.

THE BIG SLEEP

The bear is not a true hibernator, as its body cools during winter by a mere 9°F (5°C) or so from its normal temperature of around 90°F (32°C)—even though the temperature in the den may be close to freezing. In fact, some sleeping bears shiver to keep warm; this reflex is denied to true hibernators, who also cannot be roused from sleep. On warm winter days, the American black bear may awaken and leave the den for a few hours. If undisturbed, however, it may sleep for a full month without moving. During its sleep, the bear

Wayne Lankinen/Bruce Coleman Ltd.

Judd Cooney/Oxford Scientific Films

No slouch when it comes to climbing, the black bear will readily shin up a trunk to nap in a comfortable fork between branches.

EXCAVATING

soil from beneath the spreading roots of a tree (above) *often provides a snug den for a black bear.*

Although sheltered, the bear generally has a good view of its surroundings from a temporary resting place (left).

in SIGHT

DENNING LOCATIONS

The American black bear makes use of a variety of locations for its den. Caves or well-sheltered crevices among rocky outcrops are popular sites, as are hollow trees or logs, or among the roots of a fallen tree. The bear enlarges hollow trees by scraping away at the walls—the resulting wood chips help to make the bed cozy—and it may drag vegetation into a cave to achieve the same result. Sometimes a bear digs into the slope of a hillside to hollow out a chamber as a den, and in the Hudson Bay area, individuals sometimes dig into a snowbank. It seems that female black bears often den in small compartments where the entrance, in particular, is too small for males to enter. Bears have been known to return to the same den in successive years.

uses about half the energy it consumes when active, and its heart rate slows considerably.

Just how long the bear sleeps depends on the location. Those in northern Canada and Alaska, for example, go to their dens earlier and for longer than bears farther south. Usually they are asleep in their dens from October until late April. Down south in Idaho, denning may occur from November until late March or early April. In southeastern states such as Florida, some bears do not sleep at all. Right across the range, if a bear has insufficient fat reserves to last the winter, it, too, may not den.

THE HEART RATE OF ONE SLEEPING BEAR WAS TIMED AT 8 BEATS PER MINUTE, AS OPPOSED TO 50–80 DURING ACTIVE MONTHS

Usually the bear stops feeding a few days before denning, during which time it becomes lethargic and its stomach shrinks and stiffens. Some bears feed finally on resinous roughage, such as leaves and pine needles; they even tug out and eat tufts of their own fur. This passes through the digestive system to form a short anal plug in the rectum. The purpose of this is unclear, although while asleep the bear passes no waste matter. The bear voids this anal plug soon after leaving the den in spring.

When the bear does emerge, thin and gaunt, it takes a few weeks for its metabolic rate to return to normal, allowing it to eat its usual daily intake of food. Often the black bear continues to lose weight for another month or two after leaving the den. ∎

LIFE CYCLE

Black bears usually mate between June and mid-July, or a little later in northern areas. Now males wander the range in search of females; if they meet a rival, particularly in the vicinity of a female, a fight may break out. The female remains in estrus until she has been mated; males and females spend little time with each other even at this time, usually mating and then parting again.

Birth will take place when the mother is in her den during the winter sleep, where the tiny cubs are protected during their first few months. To achieve this timing, the fertilized egg is not

---

THE FERTILIZED EGG ENTERS THE UTERUS, PERHAPS DIVIDES A FEW TIMES, THEN FLOATS FREE FOR A FEW MONTHS

---

implanted in the female's uterus until around October, often when she is already denning, and true gestation takes eight to ten weeks from this time. If, by any chance, the female has not put down sufficient fat reserves to nourish her and the potential litter, the egg does not implant but simply gets reabsorbed into her body.

POCKET-SIZED CUBS

In January or February, the female gives birth to up to five, but usually two or three, cubs, rousing herself just sufficiently to bite through the umbilical cords. The cubs are incredibly tiny, weighing less than 1/500th of the mother's weight. They are blind, helpless, and covered in such fine, sparse hair that they actually look naked. For the next few weeks, they simply nestle into their sleeping mother's fur and suckle her rich milk. Their eyes open at 25–30 days old.

At first, the cubs' hindquarters are so weak that if they want to move around the den, they have to pull themselves along by their forelegs. They develop fairly rapidly, however, and by the

FROM BIRTH TO DEATH

AMERICAN BLACK BEAR

GESTATION: 220 DAYS INCLUDING DELAYED IMPLANTATION

LITTER SIZE: 1–5, USUALLY 2 OR 3

BREEDING: MAY–JUNE

WEIGHT AT BIRTH: 8–10 OZ (248–312 G)

EYES OPEN: 25–30 DAYS

FIRST WALKING: 5 WEEKS

WEANED: 6–8 MONTHS

INDEPENDENCE: 13–14 MONTHS

SEXUAL MATURITY: 4–5 YEARS IN FEMALE, 5–6 YEARS IN MALE

LONGEVITY: HARD TO ASSESS, BUT 26 YEARS RECORDED

MATING

is one of the few times that males and females meet—and then only briefly. Come autumn, the female retires to her den, where she will later give birth.

EARLY SUMMER

heralds the breeding season, when sexually mature males compete aggressively to secure their mating rights.

YOUNG ADULTS

set out in their second spring to live life on their own. Times can be tough, as they must defer to mature adults at prime feeding sites.

Illustrations Joanne Cowne

254

GROWING UP

The life of a young black bear

IN THE SPRING

the new family emerges from the den, the cubs now fully developed. They stay close to their mother, who protects them from marauding adult bears. Time is spent nursing, sleeping, and playing rough-and-tumble games with one another.

● **A female American black bear may be mated by several bears during the weeks she is in estrus.**

● **A human baby having the same weight proportion as the American black bear to its mother at birth would weigh only about 5 oz (140 g).**

● **Most female bears produce one cub in their first litter and two or more in later seasons.**

● **American black bear cubs in the same litter may display different coat colors.**

time they are five weeks old, they are strong enough to walk. By the time the mother awakens, her cubs are fully furred, miniature bears, ready to accompany her and examine the world around them.

The female is fiercely protective of her young at this time, and they are indeed vulnerable. It is, in fact, adult male bears—black and brown (grizzly)—that present the greatest danger. The cubs also fall prey to pumas, bobcats, and eagles. Their mother tries to protect them by leaving them in a sheltered

> THE TWO MONTHS AFTER THEY FIRST LEAVE THE DEN ACCOUNT FOR THE GREATEST MORTALITY AMONG CUBS

nest, either in the undergrowth or a hollow tree, while she goes off to forage for food. She, after all, is in a weakened state after her sleep and must get sufficient food so that she can nourish her cubs.

The cubs nurse frequently from the mother until they are six to eight months old. She usually lies on her back or her side while they suckle, but sometimes she simply sits back on her haunches and the cubs perch in her lap. Although weaned by the autumn after their birth, the cubs generally spend the following winter with their mother in the den. The next spring, the female may forcibly evict them from her territory—particularly any young males—as she once more seeks a mate.

Their first year alone is a dangerous time for young black bears. They are harassed by adult bears, especially at prime feeding spots; they are consequently attracted to places where the feeding is easy, such as garbage bins and dumps. Here, they may often be shot as nuisances. ■

THE FOLLOWING

winter the cubs once more den with their mother, but they disperse the next spring to find and establish their own territories.

255

THE BEAR NECESSITIES

ALTHOUGH THE AMERICAN BLACK BEAR HAS BEEN HEAVILY HUNTED THROUGH THE CENTURIES, ITS ADAPTABILITY HAS HELPED IT TO THRIVE IN GREATER NUMBERS THAN THE OTHER NORTH AMERICAN BEARS

Bears have been an important part of human life for centuries. The walls of the caves that were home to early humans are well illustrated with images of bears, several of which look significantly larger than the bears of today. While some prehistoric bears were certainly larger than many modern species, perhaps they merely seemed larger to those early people, whose only defense against such "savage" animals was the tools they could fashion from the rocks and stones strewn around.

Throughout the ages and throughout the world there have been incidents of bear cults and bear worship, beginning with the Neanderthals in the Stone Age, from which period rock containers containing bear skulls with large limb bones protruding

---

THROUGH THE CENTURIES THE BEAR HAS BEEN WORSHIPED AS FERTILITY SYMBOL, GOD, AND DEVIL

---

from eye and mouth cavities, suggesting some sort of rite or ceremony, have been found.

Ritual ceremonies concerning bears may still persist in parts of the world. Until fairly recently the nomadic tribes of Amur, in southeastern Asian Russia, believed that the bear could affect the abundance of their crops and the provision of fish in their rivers. To insure a bountiful supply of these staples of life, the tribes held festivals at which the bear was sacrificed amid much ritualistic wailing. The animal would have been raised from a cub just for this purpose. The bear meat was then eaten at a religious feast, during which the women of the tribe wiped handmade tears from the bear's head, which was set in the place of honor at the table.

In Japan, too, the bear held a special place in certain festivals and feasts. Again the bears were

raised especially for sacrifice but would not be killed until fully grown. The Ainu tribe believed that the sacrifice brought honor to the bear, which they worshiped as the incarnation of one of the gods. They implored it to speak well of the tribe to its departed ancestors when it rejoined them, so that they would send it back to earth to be sacrificed again. The Ainu also made copious apologies for the sacrifice, promising to send the bear's spirit on its way with gifts and riches. The bear was then killed without spilling any blood and with no outward sign of pain (which would bring bad luck). It would provide another sumptuous feast.

Over the years, bears have also played a key part in the world of entertainment. Dancing bears were popular in many places—the poor animals

A hunter poses proudly for the camera, his catch strung up from a branch (right).

Stuffed bears, mountain goats, and other mute witnesses to human greed jostle with animal traps in the trophy room of an Alaskan couple (above).

Stephen J. Krasemann/Bruce Coleman Ltd.

M. Newman/FLPA

This map shows the location of both settled and scattered black bear populations.

SCATTERED
POPULATION

SETTLED
POPULATION

Scattered populations still exist as far south as California and Mexico, as well as the midwestern and southeastern states. Many of these populations comprise isolated subspecies that are losing ground as a result of human encroachment and persecution. The comparatively remote, harsh conditions in Canada and Alaska provide a secure stronghold for the black bear; there its wide-ranging populations survive in healthy numbers.

muzzled and chained, to be led by usually none-too-kindly owners to street corners, where they were made to perform tricks and "dance." In circuses the world over, bears have always found favor and again are taught to perform. As a species they are said to be quick to learn and seem to have a rudimentary appreciation of music, which allows them to pick up a tune. Fortunately, such acts involving wild animals, particularly those involving extreme cruelty, are becoming ever less popular. Increasingly people want to protect animals within a natural environment, rather than see them degraded and badly treated in an alien one.

NORTH AMERICAN BEARS
Throughout the North American continent, the three native species—the brown or grizzly bear, the polar bear, and the American black bear—have been widely hunted by humans. All were once

prime targets for so-called "sport" hunters and, like all wild animals, stood no chance against modern firearms. In addition, all three species have been hunted for meat, fur, and trophies.

The grizzly and polar bears have known greater losses than the black bear. The extra size of the grizzly made it a splendid catch for game hunters, but in addition, it has suffered hugely from the march of civilization. Not only has its habitat been reduced to make way for agriculture and urbanization—neither of which is compatible with the grizzly—but it has also been killed by farmers who regard it as a threat to their domestic livestock. It tends, too, to have adapted less easily to the "benefits" of civilization—easy food at dumps and tourist campsites—than the American black bear. Although grizzlies still occur in national parks and reserves across their range, populations have become increasingly fragmented and isolated. Whereas they once roamed the American West in the tens of thousands, it was estimated that by the end of the 1980s there were only about 1,000 left in the western United States. They are still comparatively numerous in Alaska and Canada, where there are carefully controlled hunting laws and protective legislation.

> THE GRIZZLY IS LESS OF AN OPPORTUNIST THAN THE BLACK BEAR, WITH LITTLE OR NO INCLINATION TO LIVE ALONGSIDE HUMANS

Similarly, the polar bear was seen as a prime target by hunters eager to possess one of the creamy white pelts. When its inhospitable arctic wastes became more and more invaded by humans, it suffered accordingly. At one time it was hunted from aircraft and large motorized boats, but this was stopped in the early 1970s. Now various countries limit the numbers that may be hunted, and the polar bear's conservation—which hopefully has not come too late—is widely seen as a model for saving species in peril. If the current legislative protection is taken away, this species will probably decline rapidly.

Like its fellow natives, the American black bear has been subject to hunting through the ages, for all the same reasons—meat, fur, and sport. Its fur is the prized bearskin of British soldiers' busby helmets. In 1953, 700 black bears were killed in British Columbia to provide busbies for the soldiers at Queen Elizabeth II's coronation. It is hard to believe that, even in these enlightened times, British busbies are still made with the fur of black bears. Generally, however, the commercial value of its fur has dropped considerably. Whereas in the

John Freeman/ Tony Stone Worldwide

ENDANGERED ENVIRONMENT

RISK TO THE TIMBER TRADE

The American black bear has a great liking for the cambium layer of some trees—a cylindrical layer of cells found beneath the bark. To get to this, the bear simply strips off the bark, denuding the tree as neatly as we would peel an orange.

The areas most seriously affected are the coastal timber districts of northern California, Oregon, and Washington, where bears have done literally millions of dollars' worth of damage, in particular to pine trees. In May and June the trees are stripped of bark in their hundreds, soon bringing about their death.

In the early 1940s, the Washington Forest Protection Association launched what turned out to be a prohibitively expensive campaign to get rid of the offending bears, and the animals were killed in the hundreds. The problem continued, however, for the bears that escaped the gun simply went on stripping the trees regardless of the threats facing them. The practice of culling the bears was singularly unjust, in that the animals were simply exploiting a food source that, in the wild parts of their range, occurred naturally. A more satisfactory solution had to be found to preserve both the timber industry and the offending bears.

Finally in the 1980s, a forward-thinking hunter

A BLACK BEAR SCAVENGES AT A DUMP, SEEMINGLY OBLIVIOUS TO THE BURNING RUBBISH.

CONSERVATION MEASURES

● In 1872, the U.S. Congress established the Yellowstone National Park in Wyoming, Idaho, and Montana—the nation's first national park. Formed in order to preserve the country's natural heritage, Yellowstone is an important refuge for both black and grizzly bears. It is surrounded by no less than six national forests, which provide further ideal habitat. Glacier National Park, in Montana, is another stronghold, particularly for the now rare grizzly bear.

suggested that one way to solve the problem might be to give the bears a decoy instead of killing them. He recommended feeding them at the time when the cambium was at its tastiest, and therefore at its most vulnerable. He established special feeding stations within the wooded plantations, setting out a tempting concoction of fruit pulp combined with other tasty ingredients to attract the bears.

Recognizing both the forthright sense and the success in this plan, the Washington State Department of Fish and Game decided to extend the distribution of feeding stations. The cost of feeding bears in this way was markedly less than it cost to pay bounty hunters to kill them—and furthermore, both bear and forester profited from the scheme. It could be another conservation story with a happy ending.

BEARS IN DANGER

THE AMERICAN BLACK BEAR IS NOT LISTED IN THE INTERNATIONAL UNION FOR THE CONSERVATION OF NATURE'S *RED DATA BOOK, 1990,* ALTHOUGH SOME SUBSPECIES OR LOCALIZED RACES ARE BECOMING SERIOUSLY RARE ACROSS THE BEAR'S RANGE. THOSE LISTED BELOW ARE A FEW EXAMPLES:

URSUS AMERICANUS FLORIDANUS
UNOFFICIALLY CONSIDERED THREATENED THROUGH LOSS OF HABITAT, POPULATION FRAGMENTATION, AND CULLING BY BEEKEEPERS IN ORDER TO PROTECT THEIR COMMERCE. THIS, THE EVERGLADES BEAR, IS THE LARGEST OF ALL AMERICAN BLACK BEAR RACES.

URSUS AMERICANUS LUTEOLUS
SAID TO BE IN IMMINENT DANGER OF EXTINCTION. IT ONCE RANGED FROM TEXAS TO MISSISSIPPI BUT CURRENTLY EXISTS ONLY IN A FEW RIVERINE HABITATS IN EASTERN LOUISIANA.

Ken King/Planet Earth Pictures

Judd Courtney/Oxford Scientific Films

● Conservation measures were introduced in the 1940s, when the black bear's plight came to the attention of the U.S. authorities. Numbers have since increased.

● Government provision of food sources in the 1980s has dissuaded black bears from stripping trees. This has led them out of confrontation with foresters.

mid-1970s a pelt was worth about $44, by the early 1980s its value had dropped to less than half this.

The black bear has also lost considerable tracts of habitat to forest clearance, forcing populations to withdraw into more isolated regions. Again, populations become scattered and fragmented this way, which can have an effect on ensuing generations. Even in normal circumstances, reproductive potential is fairly low in bears; some estimates put it as low as six to eight cubs per female in a lifetime. The size of a territory can have a direct bearing on how many—if any—cubs a female will produce in a year, and as populations become increasingly isolated from one another, there can also be problems in finding a mate.

Although most authorities agree that the American black bear makes few attacks on domestic livestock, it has done serious damage in cornfields and to commercial beehives, both of these being sources of its favorite foods. Beekeepers in one district in Alberta, Canada, estimated that American black bears cost them some $200,000 in 1973 alone.

SUCCESS OF NATIONAL PARKS
The effect on the American black bear of over-hunting and habitat destruction has been to scatter populations, particularly in the south and east of its range. Concern over its numbers began in the 1940s, when conservation efforts were initiated. These have been successful, and there are considerably

ALONGSIDE MAN

THE FIRST TEDDY BEAR

It is the American black bear that may be credited with being the original "teddy bear"—a role model for literally millions of toys beloved of children all over the world. This came about at the beginning of the 20th century when the President of the United States, Theodore (Teddy) Roosevelt, captured a black bear cub while on a hunting trip. An enthusiastic naturalist, he adopted the animal as a pet. As a result, a toy manufacturer in Brooklyn decided, with the president's permission, to make and market a furry, soft toy bear that became known as the teddy bear. It must surely be one of the most successful ventures in toy making of all time, and today, teddy bears are found in every corner of the globe.

Orion Press/ZEFA

Joe McDonald/Oxford Scientific Films

A playful wrestle helps cubs to hone their survival instincts in preparation for adulthood (above).

Research into the black bear's lifestyle continues in many U.S. states (left).

more black bears in the country than there were fifty years ago. In some areas numbers are thought to have doubled. Today, none of the subspecies is listed as endangered, although some are rare. In many states, laws allow controlled hunting of the American black bear in order to keep numbers to an acceptable limit.

Where the American black bear has been most successful is in the many national parks of the United States and Canada. Although it is a naturally shy animal, it has learned to overcome this in order to exploit the feeding potential left behind by tourists. As the bears roam around the garbage cans and cars in a tourist area, having apparently lost their natural fear of humans, people forget that these are wild, and potentially dangerous, animals. Park officials continually discourage tourists from feeding the bears, for when there is no more food to offer, some of the bears turn belligerent. The fact that people have been injured from time to time by hungry bears only leads to problems for the bears ultimately, and several have been shot because of this so-called nuisance factor. In addition, bears are killed in numbers on the roads that thread through protected areas. ∎

INTO THE FUTURE

Protected in part by the extensive network of national parks in the United States and Canada, the American black bear shows no sign of losing ground against the advancing tide of human civilization. On the contrary, it is burgeoning in many areas, aided by its natural resourcefulness. Although the future is uncertain for some of the localized black bear races—those in the southern states, for example—the species as a whole has taken humankind in its stride.

In character with a general public that is now realizing, if rather belatedly, the beauty and fragility of its natural heritage, people are increasingly opting to marvel at live black bears rather than at hearth rugs or stuffed trophies. Bear-watching is becoming an industry. The black bear is a friendly creature, possessing some eerily human character traits, and its young cubs are among the most charming of any infant mammal.

PREDICTION

IF YOU GO DOWN TO THE WOODS...

Although a slow breeder, the black bear is proving capable of sustaining populations both in the remote wilds and in the national parks. However, a growing international trade in bear gall bladders now presents a new threat to this species' continued survival.

National parks are not zoos, however, and they present hazards for both tourist and bear. Careless visitors who leave strong-smelling food in their campsites, or who startle an unsuspecting bear, may experience the unpredictable, and sometimes deadly, side to this carnivore's temperament. Casualties regularly occur on both sides, but the bear is usually the loser, shot to protect a panicked tourist.

The park clearing is not, however, the only danger zone for the black bear. It wins no respect from crop farmers or beekeepers when it raids or despoils their means of livelihood, despite the fact that they are effectively stockpiling some of its favorite natural food sources. There may also be cause for concern in that the Rockies hold some of the richest mineral resources in the United States: Fossil fuels, precious ores, and heavy metals are all mined in these mountains. Any expansion of mining activities must mean further depletion of the black bear's wild habitat. ■

TRACKING BY SATELLITE

Studies of some animals in the wild have often presented scientists with difficulties, particularly when the animals concerned are shy or notoriously dangerous. However, modern technology has enabled some studies to be infinitely more far-reaching than previous field studies.

As early as 1973, the U.S. National Aeronautics and Space Administration combined with the National Geographic Society in using a weather satellite to monitor movements of animals fitted with radio transmitters. Researchers tranquilized bears before attaching the miniaturized electronic packages.

An American black bear in the Yellowstone National Park was monitored in its winter den over a period of a month or so. The satellite passed over the bear's den twice a day and received information from the transmitter fitted to the bear. As a result of these experiments, scientists learned that the temperature of a denning black bear dropped only a few degrees, even when the temperature in the den itself was close to freezing.

YOGI BEAR AND FRIENDS

The black bear is the most-often sighted large carnivore in U.S. national parks. Founded in 1872, Yellowstone is the oldest and largest national park in the United States. It covers nearly 3,475 sq miles (9,000 sq km) of volcanic plateaus, mountains, hot springs, lakes and rivers, and great tracts of pine, aspen, and cottonwood forest. As well as bears, Yellowstone boasts the buffalo, bighorn sheep, grizzly bear, and coyote among its large mammals.

Illustration Steve Kingston

BROWN BEARS

RELATIONS

The brown bear is a member of the order Carnivora, which includes:

CATS

DOGS

RACCOONS

HYENAS

MUSTELIDS

D. Robert Franz/Planet Earth Pictures

NORTHERN ROVERS

BROWN BEARS, OF WHICH THE NORTH AMERICAN GRIZZLY IS THE MOST FAMOUS, ARE AMONG THE MOST WIDELY DISTRIBUTED OF MAMMALS. SADLY, THEY HAVE DISAPPEARED FROM MUCH OF THEIR FORMER RANGE

A s the shallow rapids of an Alaskan river foam over the rocks, a group of brown bears sit attentively on the banks and stony mid-river islands. All attention is focused on the torrent; suddenly one bear plunges its muzzle underwater and emerges with a wriggling salmon in its jaws. When the fish are plentiful, there may be as many as fifty brown bears along a 330-ft (100-m) stretch of river, gorging themselves on this protein-rich food.

Although the brown bear varies in size across its wide range, it is second in size to just one other land-based carnivore: its relative the polar bear. However, the brown bear—particularly the subspecies known as the grizzly—is reputed to be the fiercest and most feared of all. That it commands such respect is not surprising; it can kill an animal as large as a moose with one swipe of its paw, and, at full charge, it is a terrifying spectacle as it moves at speeds of up to 30 mph (50 km/h).

CLASSIFICATION

Bears belong to the order Carnivora, which includes cats, dogs, raccoons, hyenas, and the weasel family. The eight species of bear are contained in three genera, all within the bear family, Ursidae.

ORDER

Carnivora
(flesh-eating mammals)

FAMILY

Ursidae
(bears)

GENUS

Ursus

SPECIES

arctos

SUBSPECIES

U. a. horribilis
(grizzly)

U. a. middendorffi
(Kodiak)

U. a. arctos
(European)

U. a. yesoensis
(Hokkaido)

Perhaps because of the awesome grizzly's reputation, brown bears are most readily associated with North America, yet they once extended all around the world north of the tropics. They roamed over most of Europe, including the British Isles, west across Russia and northern Asia to Japan, and also northern Africa. In North America they ranged southward from Canada and Alaska to Mexico. Nowadays their strongholds are still Canada and Alaska, a few scattered areas of Europe—notably Russia—and isolated populations in the mountains of western Europe.

EARLY BEARS

The genus *Ursus*, to which brown bears belong, first appeared in the Pliocene epoch, 3 or 4 million years ago. By this time, bears had long begun their evolutionary history, which dates back to the early Miocene epoch (25–5 million years ago), to a small doglike animal that bore characteristics found in both dogs and bears. From this evolved the first bearlike carnivore, which scientists placed in the genus *Ursavus* and from which most of today's bears ultimately derived.

Also descending from the *Ursavus* species and making their appearance from the late Pliocene were the short-faced bears, genus *Arctodus*. The giant short-faced bear, *A. simus*, that lived during the ensuing Pleistocene epoch, is thought to have been the largest predator of the time and possibly the largest of terrestrial carnivores ever known. Its legs were notably longer and more slender than those of today's bears, indicating that it

As if its sheer size were not enough to intimidate a rival, a grizzly bares its fearsome canines (right).

David A. Ponton/Planet Earth Pictures

A grizzly awakes after an after-dinner nap, shaking off sleepiness with a yawn (above).

264

A Kodiak bear rears up, alerted by an unfamilar smell, on its native Kodiak Island, Alaska (below).

Andy Rouse/NHPA

Darell Gulin/ZEFA

probably chased after prey over some distance. Its home range was similar to that of the brown bear today in North America.

CHARACTERISTICS

All basically chunky and solid in form, brown bears vary in size from the smallest, found in southern Europe, to the largest, in Alaska's Kodiak Island. There can be more than a 3-ft (91-cm) difference in the head-and-body length of bears from these different locations, while the bears' weight may vary from as little as 155 lb (70 kg) to more than 1,650 lb (750 kg). In keeping with the heavy body, the head is broad and massive. The brown bear is immensely strong, as numbers of reports bear witness; individuals have been observed dragging carcasses of large animals, such as horses, over rough ground.

Just as the coat of the American black bear is not always black, so the long, woolly fur of the brown bear varies in color: from a silver-gray or pale buff, through a reddish or chocolate brown, to almost black. In addition, there is the distinctive "grizzled" coat of the grizzly bear. Just to make matters more confusing, most brown bears are noticeably paler in color in the spring when they molt the long guard hairs of their coats.

Brown bears may be distinguished from black bears by the noticeable hump between their shoulders. Their nonretractile claws, which are not used for climbing—these bears seldom, if ever, ascend trees—are formidable weapons used for scratching and slashing. Curved and up to 4 in (10 cm) long, they are so sharp that, it is said, if a grizzly bear has been digging for ground squirrels, it can leave a grassy meadow looking like a plowed field.

Male brown bears are generally much larger than females—up to twice the weight and 10–15 percent longer. Females have usually reached 90 percent of their body length by the time they are five years old, but take another three years to reach their full body weight. In males, it takes even longer; they are seven years old before their body length is at 90 percent and at 12 years old they are still not up to full weight. It is thought they can live to be 50 years old, although it is unlikely that any attain this age. Female brown bears in Yellowstone National Park have lived to 25 years, at which time they are still capable of bearing young.

SUPER SCENT, STUNNING SPEED

Like all bears, the brown bear has an excellent sense of smell, on which it relies above any other sense, and it will frequently halt in its tracks to sit up and sniff its surroundings. Unlike many other bears, it also has sensitive hearing. Its eyesight, however, is said to be relatively poor.

A brown bear generally shambles around its home range at a slow walk on all fours, its head swinging from side to side. It walks on the soles of its feet, like a human, but can quickly accelerate into a thundering gallop that would soon overtake a sprinting man. The bear can gallop over even the roughest rocky ground but usually only moves at this speed if fleeing from danger or in angry pursuit of an adversary. ∎

HOW MANY SPECIES?

The great variation both in size and coat color in the brown bear in its various locations has led to confusion in the past. At one time, taxonomists named more than 230 separate species and subspecies.

Nowadays, scientists endorse just one species of brown bear, *Ursus arctos*, but are still undecided about the number of subspecies. The grizzly is often given subspecies status, as are the brown bears found on the Alaskan islands of Kodiak, Shuyak, and Afognak. Locally these bears are known as "brownies." The European brown bear is classified by different sources both as *Ursus arctos* and also *U. a. arctos*. Recognized subspecies have included the Hokkaido brown bear, the red bear of northern India and the Himalayas, and the now-extinct Atlas bear, which lived in northern Africa.

Color illustrations Jeremy Simmonds/Wildlife Art Agency

THE BROWN BEAR'S FAMILY TREE

The bear family, Ursidae, has eight species in three genera. The brown bear belongs to the genus Ursus, *which also includes the polar bear, American black bear, Asian black bear, sloth bear, and sun bear. The remaining two bears, the spectacled bear and the giant panda, are contained in separate genera of their own. The giant panda has only recently been recognized as a bear.*

ASIAN BLACK BEAR

SLOTH BEAR

SUN BEAR

SPECTACLED BEAR

Illustrations Barry Croucher/Wildlife Art Agency

GIANT PANDA

RACCOON

WEASEL

BROWN BEAR
Ursus arctos
(UR-sus ARK-tos)

Second only to the polar bear in size, the brown bear is widespread, although in scattered populations, across the northern hemisphere. The best known of the brown bears, North America's grizzly, is considered one of the most vulnerable of all subspecies.

SUBSPECIES
GRIZZLY BEAR
KODIAK BEAR
EUROPEAN BROWN BEAR
HOKKAIDO BROWN BEAR

AMERICAN BLACK BEAR
Ursus americanus
(UR-sus ah-merri-CAHN-us)

POLAR BEAR
Ursus maritimus
(UR-sus marri-TEE-mus)

BEARS

DOGS

CATS

MONGOOSES

HYENAS

ALL CARNIVORES

B/W illustrations Ruth Grewcock

ANATOMY: THE GRIZZLY BEAR

The grizzly bear is huge. With a head-body-and-leg length of 5.5–9.2 ft (1.7–2.8 m), when standing upright on its hind legs, it can tower over a man. Its cousin the Kodiak bear may stand more than 12 ft (3.6 m) tall on its hind legs.

THE FOREHEAD

is wide, contrasting with the long muzzle. The small, rounded ears give surprisingly acute hearing.

THE BODY

is extremely heavy and stocky. A hump between the shoulders, made up of fat and muscle, gives added power to the forelimbs.

The grizzly has the most impressive claws of all bears—up to 4 in (10 cm) long on its forefeet. It uses these for digging, scratching, and slashing. The black bear uses its short, stout, curved claws in climbing trees, as well as foraging; surprisingly for a climbing bear, it has thick fur between the foot and toe pads. In the wholly terrestrial grizzly, the soles are only sparsely haired.

HIND FOOT   FOREFOOT

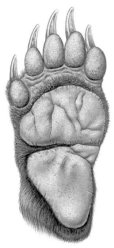
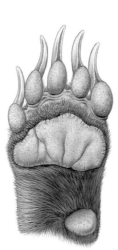

X-RAY

As with all bears, the shape of the brown bear's skeleton shows that it is built for strength rather than speed. The limb bones are stout and short in relation to body size when compared, for example, to cats or dogs. The limbs are anchors for thick muscles all along their length, giving power through a wide range of body movements. The hind feet are plantigrade (the soles are placed flat on the ground). The bear's femur strongly resembles that of humans.

BROWN BEAR SKELETON

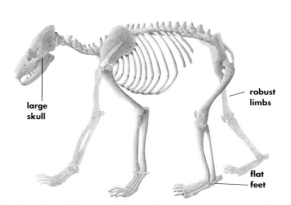

large skull

robust limbs

flat feet

The brown bear's forefeet are remarkably dextrous—the five long fingers enable it to pluck foliage and fruit with ease. The five nonretractile claws on the forefeet are particularly long and curved but are subject to a lot of wear throughout the bear's life.

FOREFOOT

X-ray illustrations Elisabeth Smith

THE GRIZZLY BEAR

CLASSIFICATION

GENUS: *URSUS*
SPECIES: *ARCTOS HORRIBILIS*

SIZE

HEAD–BODY LENGTH: 5.9–7 FT (180–213 CM)
HEIGHT TO SHOULDER: 4.3 FT (131 CM)
TAIL LENGTH: 3 IN (7.6 CM)
HINDFOOT LENGTH: 10 IN (25 CM)
FOREFOOT CLAW LENGTH: UP TO 4 IN (10 CM)
WEIGHT: 300–860 LB (136–390 KG)
WEIGHT AT BIRTH: 12–24 OZ (340–680 G)

COLORATION

VARIES FROM LIGHT CREAMY BROWN TO BROWN BLACK BUT TYPICALLY IS DARK BROWN, WITH THE LONG GUARD HAIRS "GRIZZLED" WITH WHITE TOWARD THEIR TIPS. COLORATION TENDS TO BE UNIFORM OVER THE WHOLE BODY.

FEATURES

WIDE FOREHEAD, SMALL EYES, SLIM MUZZLE. CONCAVE FACIAL PROFILE. SMALL, ROUNDED EARS, OFTEN OBSCURED BY FUR, BUT MORE VISIBLE IN SPRING AND EARLY SUMMER AFTER MOLT. CHARACTERISTIC HUMP BETWEEN SHOULDERS. LONG FORECLAWS AND CURVED TAIL. SMELL IS MOST HIGHLY DEVELOPED SENSE, BUT HEARING IS ALSO QUITE ACUTE.

THE LIPS

are quite separate from the gums, as in all bears, rendering them highly mobile.

THE FUR

varies in color but is longer and more shaggy than that of the American black bear, particularly before the spring molt. The long guard hairs on the back and shoulders of the grizzly are frosted with white at the tips, giving it the "grizzled" look that earns the bear its name.

THE LIMBS

are stocky and immensely strong. Usually the bear walks in a slow, ambling gait on all fours, but it can move at a fast, if somewhat cumbersome, gallop when necessary.

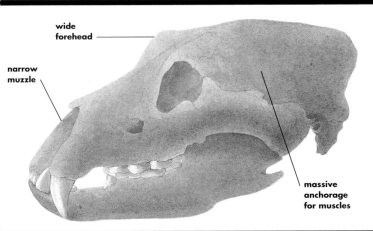

WHO'S GOT THE HUMP?

Silhouettes of the grizzly (left) and American black bear (right) reveal the grizzly's distinguishing dorsal hump.

Illustrations Steve Kingston

SKULL

All bears have long skulls when compared, for example, with cats. Bears need the extra room to accommodate grinding teeth (molars) for processing their broad diet, whereas cats, being wholly flesh-eaters, need only a few slicing teeth. To support the grinding process, a bear's skull has a heavy build on which to anchor the jaw-closing muscles.

wide forehead

narrow muzzle

massive anchorage for muscles

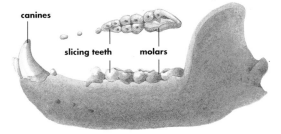

canines

slicing teeth   molars

JAWBONE

The brown bear's jawbone is heavy and powerful. Its teeth, in particular the flat-crowned molars, reflect its omnivorous diet. Its impressive upper and lower canines are used occasionally to bite and kill prey, but serve mainly in threat displays.

FISHERS AND FRUIT-EATERS

LIKE MOST BEARS, BROWN BEARS ARE NOT NATURALLY GREGARIOUS.
THE GRIZZLY MAY BE THE MOST SOCIAL OF NORTH AMERICA'S BEARS,
BUT GROUPS GENERALLY ONLY FORM AROUND A RICH FOOD SOURCE

Wherever they are found across their range, brown bears have common staple needs: finding enough food to support their large bulk, finding a mate to ensure reproduction and survival of their genes, finding shelter when needed, and avoiding predation—mainly by humans.

THE LONESOME TRAIL

The daily quest for large amounts of food, at least for much of the year, means that brown bears must often range far and wide. Inevitably this leads to a fairly solitary lifestyle, although where food is plentiful, such as a salmon stream, brown bears may gather in numbers. On such occasions,

---

BROWN BEARS CAN ADAPT WELL TO
DIFFERENT HABITATS—BUT ONLY WHERE
THEY ARE UNDISTURBED BY MAN

---

each bear is careful to observe rank. The large adult males have prime, unchallenged positions; probably next in line will be females with young cubs, and these certainly are among the most aggressive of all bears, for the maternal protectiveness is strong. Finally, lurking on the fringes, are the adolescent bears—those that have left their mothers but have yet to establish themselves as king of a range.

The search for a mate is also a lonesome quest: a male may have to wander far afield, as females may be widely dispersed. In addition, females breed only every three years—sometimes the gap is even longer—giving birth on average to two cubs in each litter. This low reproduction rate, with each female producing perhaps six to eight young in a lifetime, tends to produce aggression in an animal; in the female it is manifested in the fierce guarding of her young, while males will fight savagely for the right to mate with a receptive female. Both sexes, however, mate with as many partners as possible during breeding.

Brown bears are active at any time of the day or night. Just when they are most active depends on location, time of year, availability of food, proximity of humans, and other factors. If food is scarce, they will forage day and night, although chiefly in the mornings and evenings. If they live near human settlements, they tend to shun the daylight. They are nevertheless highly adaptable and in many areas have learned to overcome their fear of humans when advantageous to them. Brown bears have been known to take fish off the lines of fishermen struggling to land a catch, and, like the American black bear, they have learned that visitors to national parks—many of which are hosts to grizzlies—can bring easy pickings from leftover picnics in parking lots and campsites.

John Warden/Tony Stone Worldwide

This youngster (above) *has some months to go before it leaves its mother for a solitary adult life.*

A female shepherds her two young cubs in Alaska (below). They still have much to learn about life.

John Warden/Tony Stone Worldwide

D. Robert Franz/Planet Earth Pictures

The aggression bred into a brown bear's nature in order to help it in the battle for survival has led to a fierce reputation—particularly in the grizzly. Interestingly, brown bears in Eurasia seem not to have acquired the same reputation; persecuted as they have been for centuries by humans, those that have survived tend to keep out of sight of people as much as possible.

DROP THE CAMERA AND RUN!
A grizzly attacking is said to be an awesome sight, but it does not follow the popular storybook image of a bear advancing on its hind legs, its lips curled back like a snarling dog. Instead, the bear rushes toward the object of its attack on all fours, the usual shuffling, loose-skinned hulk turned into an astoundingly fast-moving, dynamic force. Its ears are pinned back and its mouth open to display the awesome canine teeth. Advice on what to do in the face of such an onslaught varies; climb a tree is one suggestion, for adult brown bears do not do this. They can, however, reach high up into the tree with their strong forepaws and claws to take a firm hold of a fleeing victim. Another recommendation is to make as much noise as possible while hitting the animal around its eyes. All options, however, require a measure of quick, cool thought that may not be readily available when 750 lb (340 kg) of bear is thundering rapidly in your direction. ■

Most bears are excellent fishers, and the brown bear is no exception.

HABITATS

E. & P. Bauer/ZEFA

In North America, brown bears occur from Alaska, south through most of British Columbia and western Alberta, to south-central Nevada. Even within these areas, they occupy a number of different types of environment, from thick woodland and forested areas to more open tundra and windswept coastlines. They are also found in and around meadows of subalpine areas.

At one stage, it seems, brown bears were common over the Great Plains to California and south into Mexico. Nowadays, their stronghold is Alaska and Canada; in the other states they exist in isolated populations, mostly in the protected national parks. More than 30 percent of brown bears found south of Canada and Alaska, for example, inhabit what is known as the Greater Yellowstone Ecosystem in Montana and Wyoming. This covers a 5.5-million-acre (2.2-million-hectare) area surrounding the Yellowstone National Park, as well as the 2.2 million acres (0.9 million hectares) of park itself. Within Montana, grizzlies are found in the Glacier National Park and Great Bear, Bob Marshall, Scapegoat, and Mission Mountains Wilderness areas. The Selkirk Mountains of Idaho and Washington also provide refuge to wild grizzlies.

The brown bears of northern British Columbia and Alaska, including the islands of Kodiak, Afognak, and Shuyak off Alaska's southern coast, are the largest in the world—even

AMAZING FACTS

● Polar bears and brown bears are so genetically similar that, in zoo experiments, they have been interbred and have produced fertile hybrids.

● It is often claimed that bears are highly intelligent animals. Although this is not conclusively proved, their brains possess several features that are similar to those found in the brains of primates. An American Indian myth relates how the grizzly was created as a more powerful and clever animal than any other.

● Brown bears have one of the lowest reproductive rates of any North American mammal.

DISTRIBUTION

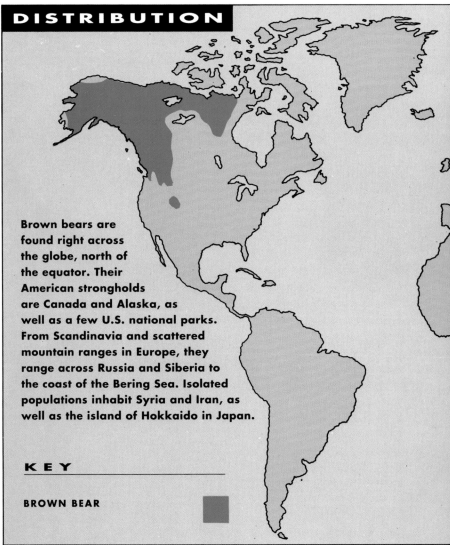

Brown bears are found right across the globe, north of the equator. Their American strongholds are Canada and Alaska, as well as a few U.S. national parks. From Scandinavia and scattered mountain ranges in Europe, they range across Russia and Siberia to the coast of the Bering Sea. Isolated populations inhabit Syria and Iran, as well as the island of Hokkaido in Japan.

KEY

BROWN BEAR

A grizzly bear looks out over its domain (left). *Adult brown bears need a huge area in which to roam in search of food, shelter, and a mate.*

A European brown bear lumbers through heavy snow looking for a meal (right). *Bears sleep through much of the winter but will rouse themselves whenever hungry.*

Reinhard Siegel/Aquila Photographics

outweighing all but the very largest polar bears. One reason for this is that their range is criss-crossed with salmon streams, full of this readily available food source that is rich in fat and protein. And there is plenty to go around. Not only can the bears gorge themselves on the salmon, but they need use little energy in catching them—both factors that help contribute to their bulk.

In Eurasia, where their range extends from Scandinavia to eastern Russia and south as far as Spain, Syria, and Iran, brown bears favor remote

BEARS BASICALLY FAVOR THE SAME HABI-TATS THAT WE DO: FERTILE VALLEYS, WOODED SLOPES, AND LUSH MEADOWS

mountain woodland, where they can live undisturbed by humans. The Himalayas, Pyrenees, and Alps, and the Cantabrian, Carpathian, and Abruzzi Mountains, have all been home to the brown bear; it is possible that they survive today in the lower wooded slopes of these areas. They also inhabit Hokkaido, the northernmost island of Japan, in the wooded mountain areas.

Brown bears were once common in the formerly wooded areas of North Africa. Deforestation is not a new practice; the forests of northern Africa were largely felled by the Romans to support the needs of their great empire. As this happened, the brown bears withdrew into the partially wooded, mountainous regions of Morocco and Algeria, becoming extinct from there only at the end of the 19th century.

273

Across its current range, the brown bear will make seasonal migrations to visit rich food sources. Salmon streams are of interest when they are full of salmon traveling back to their spawning grounds; when berries are abundant in lightly wooded areas, bears will travel considerable distances to exploit them. At other times, they take to more open ground to dig out ground-dwelling, burrowing rodents and small mammals.

Just as the American black bear leaves evidence of its presence, so too does the grizzly. Overturned rocks—often of some size—fruit-bearing bushes pulled apart and pillaged, logs ripped into with deep claw marks, and similar scratches—often very high up—as well as tooth marks and stripped patches on tree trunks, all indicate that brown bears have passed by. Where they have dug for rodents, there may be large holes, surrounded by mounds of soil. Another clue is a carcass hidden in a shallow scrape and loosely covered with earth and vegetation. In this instance, the bear will not be far away, so trackers would do well to retreat to a safe distance!

Brown bears will often make a daytime bed, usually under cover of dense undergrowth. They either flatten the vegetation with their heavy bodies or hollow out an oval depression in the

FOCUS ON

THE CARPATHIANS

Forming a vast horseshoe of peaks and plateaus through eastern Europe, the Carpathian range is one of Europe's last mountain wildernesses. From the Czech Republic in the northwest, the Carpathians arc south and east through Poland and Ukraine, finally twisting sharply to the west in Romania to form the Transylvanian Alps.

Average altitudes are far lower than those of the European Alps, and much of the Carpathian range is characterized by hilly plains clothed in undisturbed forests. The vegetation is, however, basically alpine by nature, varying with the altitude. The deciduous forests of the lower slopes, where brown bears roam, give way higher up to conifers and alpine meadows.

The Carpathians are home to one of Europe's few surviving wolf populations. In summer, the wolves follow the cattle, sheep, and goats as they are herded up to the high meadows. Come the heavy winter snows, however, they descend the slopes and revert to their natural prey of roe deer and wild boar. The lynx preys locally on the young deer, as well as hares, susliks, and ground birds. One of the most majestic predators is the golden eagle, which nests in the rocky peaks and swoops down to kill mammals and birds.

VEGETATION ZONES

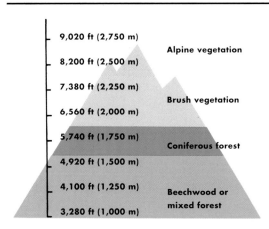

9,020 ft (2,750 m)

Alpine vegetation

8,200 ft (2,500 m)

7,380 ft (2,250 m)

Brush vegetation

6,560 ft (2,000 m)

5,740 ft (1,750 m)

Coniferous forest

4,920 ft (1,500 m)

4,100 ft (1,250 m)

Beechwood or mixed forest

3,280 ft (1,000 m)

The graded altitudes of a mountain have a significant effect on the climate and plant life at its various levels. Forest predominates in the Carpathians, which enjoy a continental climate owing to their great distance from any oceans. On the highest ground, however, trees are small and scarce.

ground, some 1 ft (30 cm) wide and 4 ft (122 cm) long. This they may line with leaves or other soft vegetation. Routes that brown bears habitually take through undergrowth will show as trampled trails, and often their footprints are easily discernible in soft ground. The hind prints can be enormous—1 ft (30 cm) long and 8 in (20 cm) wide, with foreprints being as wide but only half as long, the long claws printing well ahead of the toe pads. The stride is about 2 ft (61 cm) at a walk—up to four times this if the bear is galloping. ∎

NEIGHBORS

Over much of their range, the Carpathians are barely inhabited by humans. Having largely escaped the effects of the last Ice Age, their wild woods have long been a refuge for wildlife.

SNOW FINCH

In winter, this high-mountain species generally moves to the lower forests where the bear lives.

CHAMOIS

The graceful chamois is a fairly common sight in the wooded slopes and high alpine pastures.

Neighbor illustrations Edwina Goldstone/Wildlife Art Agency

Reinhard Siegel/Aquila Photographics

THE CARPATHIANS

This mountain range (shown left as dark green) arcs through some 800 miles (1,300 km) of eastern Europe. The bulk of the range lies within Romania. The western ranges drain away to the Baltic Sea, while the southern and eastern ranges drain into the Black Sea, via the Danube, Dniester, and other rivers.

POLAND

HUNGARY

ROMANIA

MOUNTAIN HARE

This inhabitant of higher elevations is similar to the brown hare but is a little smaller and stockier.

GOLDEN EAGLE

Among the most beautiful of the birds of prey, this bird may be seen soaring over the highest peaks.

COMMON FROG

The common frog inhabits alpine areas as well as moorland and marshes, wherever there is water.

SWALLOWTAIL BUTTERFLY

The beautiful markings of this butterfly act as a defense, deflecting attack away from its body.

FIRE SALAMANDER

The range of this brightly patterned amphibian extends across Europe and into North Africa.

FOOD AND FEEDING

Brown bears spend much of their time foraging for food to fuel their sizable bulk. Although they eat both flesh and plant food, the mainstays of their diet vary according to both season and location, depending on what is available.

EATING FOR HEALTH

For all brown bears, vegetable matter makes up the bulk of the annual intake—usually as much as 70 to 80 percent. But as their digestive tract and system is not like that of herbivores—that is, adapted to breaking down and fermenting the cellulose in vegetable matter—they must look for plant food that is as high as possible in easily extracted nutritive value, such as roots and fruits, rather than rely on a large intake of grass and leaves.

In North America in the spring, for example, their choice of plant food tends to be roots and bulbs, backed up by grasses and mosses. As spring progresses into summer, they are likely to feed more on the newly sprouting vegetation. Come the autumn, acorns, fungi, and berries of all descriptions become important and widely sought after.

BEARS TEND TO SCAVENGE CARRION MORE IN THE EARLY SPRING, WHEN THERE IS LESS VEGETATION AVAILABLE

All brown bears will include flesh in their diet whenever the opportunity arises. Their long claws make light work of digging burrowing rodents, such as ground squirrels, marmots, and mice, from their burrows. They also search out insects and their grubs and, like other bears, raid bees' nests for the bees and larvae as well as the honey.

HUNTING AND FISHING

In some areas brown bears are active hunters and have been known to prey quite regularly on hoofed mammals, including domestic livestock. In the arctic areas of Alaska and Canada, for example, they prey on caribou and other ungulates; a contest of speed between the two animals would never favor the bear, so instead it tends to wait and ambush the victim as it approaches the water to cross or drink. The bear attacks by swiping at the animal with a vicious paw and sinking its long, sharp canines into the back of the neck to deal a mortal blow.

An animal the size of a caribou represents several meals to a brown bear, so the bear will drag it to a sheltered spot where it covers it with dirt and

leaves, returning to feast on it as it feels the need. However, when it has such a cache as this, it rarely strays far away from it.

Bears that live near the coast or by rivers include all manner of aquatic life in their diet. Seaweed, crabs, shellfish, and washed-up bodies of sea mammals are all food to beach-foraging bears.

Illustration Priscilla Barrett/Wildlife Art Agency

GONE FISHING

One fishing technique is to stand at the top of a small waterfall and attempt to catch the fish as they leap upstream.

DIGGING

for dinner. Brown bears are extremely dexterous, using their forepaws to gather fruit and acorns and to dig up roots.

Trout and other fish are also favored fare, as are beavers, which are hard to catch but high in nutrients. There is no doubt, however, that to those bears that live near the salmon rivers of Canada, southern Alaska, and northeastern Siberia, the spawning salmon represent the greatest treat of all.

Congregating on the riverbanks and midstream islands, the usually solitary bears may be found in large numbers at this time; up to 50 or 60 may be grouped in one fairly small area. Fishing techniques vary between bears and seem to be a wholly individual matter, not always learned by watching others. Some wait in the shallows and pin a passing fish to the streambed with a huge paw; others plunge into the deeper water from a midstream rock, grabbing a fish in their jaws. Others wade through the shallow water, dipping their muzzle below the surface to look for fish, which, again, they catch in their jaws.

The brown bear has extremely dexterous paws. It holds a salmon in its forepaws, while peeling off the skin with its teeth. Equally, it will readily use its paws to gather fruit and acorns from the undergrowth. ■

in SIGHT

FOOD FIGHTS

On the northern coastline of North America, the ranges of the brown bear and the American black bear overlap, so the two species compete for food.

Brown bears are larger and more aggressive than black bears and, indeed, have been known to prey on them. Although the diet of the two bears is similar, brown bears have the advantage of long claws, which enable them to dig more successfully for roots and tubers, as well as burrowing rodents. However, their larger bulk means they also need to eat more; as a result, they tend to be active for longer, often foraging when the black bears are resting.

BLACK BEAR RANGE

BROWN BEAR RANGE

OVERLAP OF RANGE

CARRION

carrying. The carcass of prey or carrion is often dragged away to a favorite spot, where it is covered and later feasted on.

TERITORY

Brown bears are no more sociable than other bears, tending to gather in numbers only where there is a rich food source. They occupy a home range, which varies in size in differing locations; where food sources are thin on the ground, for example, a bear will need a larger range.

HOME ON THE RANGE

The home range of an adult male is usually much larger than that of a female. Because ranges usually overlap, males and females often have several prospects from which to choose and often mate with multiple partners. Depending on the availability of food, a North American adult male's range can vary from 9.5 to 386 sq mi (24.5 to 1,000 sq km). Bears living in coastal areas generally have smaller home ranges than those inland.

Because a female usually mates with more than one male when she is in breeding condition, it is not unusual for litters to contain cubs from separate sires. Because of the competition with other females, however, each female appears to maintain a range exclusive of other females, although occasionally her female offspring may stay in the vicinity after the rest of the family has dispersed. The home range of adult males may overlap, for bears are not aggressively territorial except in the mating season. By and large, they neither mark nor defend the area in which they spend their time.

In Europe and Asia, a brown bear's home range is often immense; in Sweden, for example, it may be twice that—up to 835 sq mi (2,163 sq km)—of its North American cousins. Bear populations are much lower in Sweden, so perhaps the males have to wander over huge distances to find a breeding partner.

Wherever they live, brown bears do not strictly migrate. However, they may travel widely with the passing seasons, in order to exploit fresh food sources. In autumn, for example, when the bears need to fatten up to survive the winter, they will move to areas where there are supplies of berries.

BEAR FIGHTS

Solitary to the last detail, bears communicate with one another as little as possible. The main interaction will be between siblings that play together as cubs, learning skills, such as fighting, which they will need in deadly earnest in adult life. These play-fights follow a pattern: The bears rear on their hind legs and wrap their forelimbs

T. Bledsoe/Oxford Scientific Films

Two young Kodiak bears jaw playfully in a river (above), *practicing the skills they will later need for hunting.*

NOMADIC LIFE

Males (above right) *are solitary. They move in and out of mainly female territory and can be a menace to cubs.*

Illustration Guy Troughton/Wildlife Art Agency

EASE THAT ITCH

A brown bear rubs its back against a tree to dislodge annoying parasites (right).

MOTHER LOVE

The female guards her young, warding off intruders, including adult males (below).

DENNING

In all but the most southerly parts of its range, the brown bear spends most of the winter asleep in a den—either a cave or an excavated hollow. It stocks up on food sources in the autumn, building up a thick layer of fat under its skin.

As in all bears, the brown bear is not a true hibernator. On warm days, it may awaken and leave the den for a few hours. However, it generally does not eat or expel waste while denning.

When it emerges in spring, the bear may weigh less than half of its final autumn weight. Weak and hungry, it tends to stay close to the den for a few weeks before its strength and weight return.

around one another while "jawing"—gaping the mouth to show their large canine teeth—which acts as a warning of their weaponry, and shaking the head from side to side and growling gently. As adults, two males will jaw and growl as a prelude to fighting. If neither retreats at this stage, they usually pull away and then charge at one another, snapping with the jaws, swiping with the heavy paws, and raking with the vicious claws.

A BROWN BEAR MAY DISPLAY A STRONGLY INDIVIDUAL TEMPERAMENT, WHICH IS USUALLY DEVELOPED EARLY IN ITS LIFE

With many carnivores, such as the cats and dogs, the tail is used to convey mood. When two rival male cats circle each other warily, whipping their tails from side to side, the atmosphere is clearly hostile. A bear's tiny tail is little use in this regard, however. It is likely instead that facial expression, along with the tilt of the head, neck, and ears, gives clues to how a bear is feeling. This is probably why confrontations start with jawing.

An angry bear presses back its ears and reveals the whites of its eyes. If its ears are pricked forward, the bear is alert and listening. Brown bears are less vocal than American black bears; possibly the natural forest habitat of the latter, where visibility is necessarily restricted, makes it necessary for them to keep in touch through sound rather than sight. However, brown bears will growl and roar when angry or challenging another bear or a human, and a female will keep in touch with her cubs by calling to them. ■

LIFE CYCLE

Brown bears mate from May or June to July, and it is at this time of year that males start searching around their territories for receptive females. As female brown bears generally only mate every three years, they are in comparative short supply, and angry fights may break out between competing adult males at this time.

It is the act of mating that induces ovulation in the female, so she will mate several times while she is in estrus, sometimes with just one male, but usually with two or three. For this reason, a male may often attempt to hide a receptive female away for a week or so, keeping her away from other males and mating with her as many times as possible. A male will try to mate with several females during the spring mating season.

DELAYED IMPLANTATION

Like some other mammals, bears experience a delayed implantation of the fertilized egg into the wall of the uterus. Implantation occurs in October or November—that is, after the female has fed herself up in the autumn and has actually begun her winter sleep. (A pregnant female generally enters her den earlier in the winter and emerges later in the spring than other bears.) True gestation begins with implantation of the egg, and the tiny cubs, weighing no more than 12–24 oz (340–680 g), are born about three months later, while the female is still asleep in the den.

A litter may contain up to four cubs, but usually two or three. Tiny, naked, blind, and helpless, they remain in the den for a few months, feeding on their mother's rich milk. Next to polar bears, the milk of brown bears is the richest of all bears' milk, and contains up to 33 percent fat. It is also rich in protein, so the cubs gain weight rapidly.

The female bear is not feeding at this time, which is another reason why she must put on sufficient weight during the autumn and why it is important that she expend no energy in any other way. When she emerges from the den with her cubs—now fully furred and wholly recognizable

GROWING UP
The life of a young brown bear

MATING

occurs from May to July. Once the male has found a receptive female, there is a brief courtship before mating occurs. The implantation of the egg is delayed until the late autumn.

THE YOUNG

stay with their mother for over two years. After this time, the female young may stay nearby, but the males leave to establish their own range.

WHY ARE BEAR CUBS SO TINY?

THE DEN

is either a natural hollow tree or a specially dug burrow. The young, born in early spring, are nearly naked and helpless.

All bears give birth to cubs that weigh only a tiny fraction of their own body weight. This is because they are born—and develop—when their mother is sleeping. In most mammals, a pregnant, and then nursing, female needs to feed on richer food than at any other time of her life. In addition, for the first few months of their lives, the female bear must also provide her cubs' only nourishment—still while she is not feeding. Although we can only speculate, it is likely that the female conserves more energy with a shorter pregnancy and her ability to produce small cubs with independent thermoregulation.

L. Lee Rue/Frank Lane Picture Agency

IN LATE SPRING

the mother emerges from her den, together with her cubs. Though playful, they remain close by her side.

as baby bears—she will keep them close to her and guard them fiercely. Adult male brown bears are one of the main predators at this time of the cub's life. Besides providing the adult with a nutritious meal, there are two other possible reasons for this. First, by killing young males, an adult male reduces the number of brown bears likely to compete for females in the future; and second, without a litter, the female will come back into estrus the following year, thereby providing another opportunity for mating.

LEARNING THE ROPES

Provided that they survive, the cubs will stay with their mother for at least the next two years, learning how to forage and hunt by following her closely. Play-fighting teaches them the skills they will need for survival on their own.

Although they are usually weaned at about five months old, brown bear cubs may go on suckling occasionally from their mother right up to the time that the family disperses. This probably helps to maintain the strong bond between a female and her cubs. When the time comes for them to leave, the female offspring will often stay nearby, but young males may wander widely, as far as 60 mi (100 km) from their birthplace. ■

FROM BIRTH TO DEATH

BROWN BEAR

MATING SEASON: MAY–JULY

GESTATION: 80–226 DAYS, BUT IMPLANTATION OF EGG IS DELAYED UNTIL OCTOBER–NOVEMBER. BORN APPROXIMATELY 80 DAYS POST-IMPLANTATION.

LITTER SIZE: 1–4

WEANED: ABOUT 5 MONTHS, BUT MAY GO ON SUCKLING OCCASIONALLY FOR UP TO 2 YEARS

LONGEVITY: 15–34 YEARS IN THE WILD; UP TO 50 YEARS IN CAPTIVITY

Illustration Evi Antoniou

LOSING GROUND

ACROSS MOST OF THEIR WIDE RANGE, THE HABITATS OF BROWN BEARS HAVE BECOME INCREASINGLY FRAGMENTED. THE RESULTING ISOLATED POPULATIONS IN MANY AREAS ARE AT CONSIDERABLE RISK

O f all the world's wild animals, bears have always occupied a special place in our culture. When Stone Age humans faced the bear in a contest, doubtless the odds favored the powerful, savage bears. However, long before modern humans outstripped the bear completely with firearms, their superior intelligence and weight of numbers in a hunt tilted the balance of power in their favor. Furthermore, humans began to see the bear as more than simply a dangerous wild animal: one that, while threatening their survival at times, also provided them with food, warm clothing, entertainment, and possibly wealth.

As early as the first century B.C., Roman emperors demanded the capture of huge numbers of brown bears to fight with gladiators and dogs in the sports arena. In 61 B.C., 100 brown bears were taken to Italy for this purpose, while nearly two centuries later, the emperor Gordian is said to have used nearly 1,000 bears in a single blood-thirsty spectacle. The evil practice of bearbaiting—in which bears were often blinded, chained to a stake, and then set upon by dogs while spectators goaded them with sticks and whips—began in ancient times and was finally stopped in Britain only in the 19th century. Indeed, so popular was it in Britain that it was one of the most enduring of entertainments from the time of the Norman Conquest until the 18th century.

DANCING IN THE STREET

Not all the ways in which bears have been used for entertainment over the centuries are as blood-thirsty as those mentioned, although whether they have actually been any less cruel is highly debatable. Bears have long been star turns in circuses, trained to do all manner of performances and tricks. So popular have they been that "bear academies" became a feature of some countries—Russia, for example; here captive brown bears were kept and "trained" for circuses and entertainment. Often the methods used were highly dubious, and the academies were finally outlawed.

Bears as street entertainers were once a common sight, both in Europe and along the U.S. eastern seaboard. Bears—frequently brown bears—were captured, probably as cubs, and then taught to "dance" in a crude fashion; that is, to shuffle one hind foot to the other. Often they were dressed in outlandish costumes, only adding to the debasement of the spectacle. Training methods in these instances were equally questionable—there have been reports of bears being taught to dance

Herbert Schwind/Okapia/Oxford Scientific Films

People still pay to be amused by dancing bears, sustaining the market for such cruelty (above).

This map shows the former and present distribution of the brown bear.

/// **FORMER DISTRIBUTION**

■ **PRESENT DISTRIBUTION**

Across Europe and Asia, brown bears have experienced a contraction in the southern parts of their range. In southern Europe, they survive only in isolated populations in remote, mountainous areas.

The situation is similar in North America, with Alaska and Canada remaining the most secure retreats for the species. There are few bears to be found in the central and southern states.

by placing hot trays beneath their feet as music is played, so that an association forms in the bear's mind between music and pain. Also, as the bears got bigger and therefore potentially more dangerous, they would be restrained by such methods as piercing a hole through their upper lip or nose into which a ring would be inserted.

Although it is now illegal to own a bear caught in the wild in many of the countries where this entertainment was once popular, there are still a number of dancing bears in some European countries—Greece and Turkey, for example. Such practices can, in reality, be extremely difficult to outlaw by authorities; it is hard to prove that the animal was caught in the wild, and often the authorities have no place to put a bear should

Bearskins for sale in Turkey. The hide is sold as a rug or a wall hanging.

Ardea

ENDANGERED SPECIES

they take it. Turning a blind eye becomes the most expedient way of dealing with the situation. The most effective way of stopping such practices, however, is if the perpetrators find no audience.

BEAST OF MYTH AND LEGEND

Perversely, just as humans have persecuted bears for centuries, they have also worshiped them. Countless myths and legends from cultures all over the world surround bears; many of them involve bears who could turn into people or vice versa, displaying the wisdom and knowledge, as well as the strength, of both animals. The fact of the bear's "hibernation," when it appeared to return from the dead to be reborn each spring, not only displayed its empathy with nature but seemed to endow it with almost supernatural qualities. The ancient Greeks, Hindus, Inuit, and tribespeople of western Siberia all have legends surrounding the bear constellations, Great Bear and Little Bear—Ursa Major and Ursa Minor— displayed in the night sky of the northern hemisphere. Bears have also always featured in western literature. They have been both the heroes and villains of fairy tales told the world over, and in the 20th century, they are known to thousands of children from such characters as Winnie the Pooh, Paddington Bear, and Rupert Bear.

THE CREE TRIBE HAD MANY NAMES FOR THE BEAR, SUCH AS "ANGRY ONE," "BIG GREAT FOOD," AND "FOOD OF THE FIRE"

In many countries, even as the bear was being hunted and killed, so ceremonies were held in its honor and to placate its spirit. One such event featured the Ainu tribe of Japan, who share the brown bears' home of Hokkaido. Although these people would kill bears with poisoned arrows as part of their hunting, they would also hold a ritualistic annual festival when a hand-reared bear would be killed and eaten in a four-day ceremony.

PERSECUTION

In far more areas, of course, the hunting and killing of the brown bear has carried with it no such apparent niceties of feeling and conscience. Right across its range, the brown bear has come into conflict with farmers, who see it as a threat to their livestock, and others who perceive it either as an object of sport or as a danger to themselves and their families. In Japan, again, the brown bear has long been an animal with a price on its head, rather than one to protect. Bounties are possibly still offered by communities apparently plagued by

Main Picture Stephen Krasemann/ZEFA

THE GRIZZLY

Today, some 90 percent of North America's population of brown bears are found in Alaska, the Yukon, the Rocky Mountains of Alberta and British Columbia, and the mainland Northwest Territories. There may be fewer than 1,000, possibly only 600, brown bears— the grizzlies—in the 48 states to the south of Canada.

Two centuries ago, there were thought to be 50,000 to 100,000 grizzly bears widely dispersed across the western half of the United States, south to central Mexico. Then the settlers arrived, ready to drive their cattle across the land and build themselves homes. Instantly there was a conflict between them and what until that time had been the virtually undisputed wild king of the plains—the grizzly bear. Seeing this savage wild animal as a predator on their livestock, the ranchers gave it no chance. Grizzlies were shot, trapped, lassoed, and poisoned in the thousands, until, less than 100 years later, they had more or less gone from the plains altogether.

In California, the apparently distinctive subspecies *Ursus arctos californicus* had disappeared from the state altogether by 1922. In less than 60 years, it had gone from a reasonable abundance to extinction. Just 10 years later, Mexico's grizzly —*Ursus arctos nelsoni*, small by brown-bear standards, but nonetheless the

LIKE THE WOLF, THE GRIZZLY BEAR (*RIGHT*) HAS BEEN DRIVEN FAR DOWN THE PATH TOWARD EXTINCTION BY HUMAN FEAR AND PARANOIA.

CONSERVATION MEASURES

● In 1963, the World Wide Fund for Nature (WWF) raised money to provide a refuge for brown bears. Ironically, this corresponded almost exactly with the date they became extinct in Mexico.

● In 1975, the grizzly was finally declared threatened under the U.S. Endangered Species Act. By this time, however, 98 percent of these bears in the United States had been destroyed.

state's largest native animal—had been hunted, trapped, and poisoned to the brink of extinction. It was known locally as the silver bear, and there were thought to be some 30 bears left in the isolated Cerro Compaño, Santa Clara, and Sierro del Nido mountain ranges until the early 1960s. Now, there are probably none left at all.

Today the map of the grizzly's distribution in the United States looks very different from 200 years ago; instead of a solid range across at least half the country, there are now a few isolated patches, mainly corresponding to the national parks and reserves. In some of these, it is thought the populations may be too small, or already too interbred, to make continued reproduction viable. Instead of being the "fierce untouchable majesty," the grizzly is viewed as one of the most vulnerable species on earth.

John Warden/Tony Stone Worldwide

Inset picture David E. Myers/Tony Stone Worldwide

● The grizzly is protected across its remaining habitat, particularly in the national parks and reserves where it is also closely studied and monitored. However, there is a persistent need to educate visitors to these parks; their ignorance often leads to dangerous conflicts with bears, and it is inevitable that the bear suffers. Usually it is shot because it is "dangerous."

BROWN BEARS IN DANGER

NORTH AMERICAN BROWN BEAR POPULATIONS, AND EUROPEAN POPULATIONS EXCEPT THAT OF RUSSIA, ALL COME UNDER APPENDIX II OF CITES (THE CONVENTION ON INTERNATIONAL TRADE IN ENDANGERED SPECIES). THIS APPENDIX INCLUDES "ALL SPECIES WHICH, ALTHOUGH NOT NECESSARILY NOW THREATENED WITH EXTINCTION, MAY BECOME SO UNLESS TRADE IN SPECIMENS OF SUCH SPECIES IS SUBJECT TO STRICT REGULATION."

THE FOLLOWING SPECIES IS LISTED IN THE *RED DATA BOOK* OF THE INTERNATIONAL UNION FOR THE CONSERVATION OF NATURE (IUCN):

MEXICAN SILVER GRIZZLY   EXTINCT

the bears, and some 400 bears were killed annually until very recently. Now it also faces constant erosion of its habitat as forests are cleared for the continuing spread of civilization.

Across its Eurasian range, the persecution of the brown bear has been fairly wholesale and its numbers are widely decimated. In all cases it is a combination of habitat destruction and generalized hunting and killing that has brought the bears to their current critical state—extinct in many areas where they once roamed freely. They survived in the British Isles no later than the 12th century, while their stay of execution lasted in North Africa until the latter part of the 19th century, and to the mid-20th century in the Arabian Peninsula and the Near East. They have disappeared from huge tracts in the remainder of their range, particularly in Europe, where they are found in increasingly small numbers in widely

TO THIS DAY, BEAR-PAW STEW REMAINS ON THE MENU OF A SELECT FEW RESTAURANTS IN THAILAND

fragmented populations. Their one stronghold is in Russia, where they are still both widespread and locally abundant, although the pressures of encroachment on their habitats and exploitation of local resources are seen as real threats.

One subspecies of brown bear in Russia has apparently already died out, although no one can actually verify its one-time existence. Classified as *Ursus arctos piscator*, it is said to have been at least the size of the Kodiak brown bear and lived on the Kamchatka Peninsula. Rumors abounded of its presence, but there were no authenticated reports—the nearest being that of a Swedish naturalist who, in 1936, apparently photographed

ALONGSIDE MAN

WILD NEIGHBORS

The brown bear receives protection in the national parks and reserves, but as a result of thoughtless visitors either leaving food lying around or actively trying to feed bears, individual animals have become "conditioned"—that is, they have grasped the connection between people and food.

In many areas, these bears have no qualms about approaching people for food. If none is offered, a bear will react in the only way it knows: aggressively. In some areas it will simply raid picnic areas; in other instances it gives chase.

In spite of its often cuddly image, the bear is still a wild animal; the only way that bear and humans can coexist in close proximity is if humans remember this and observe the rules.

David C. Fritts/Oxford Scientific Films

A grizzly sow leads her cub through Denali National Park, Alaska (above), *to the obvious delight of tourists.*

Jeff Foott/Survival Anglia

huge bear footprints in the snow and was also presented with "a pelt which far surpasses every other bearskin I have ever seen."

In the United States, the American Indians revered the bear. Although many tribes hunted it on the plains, some would not do so, seeing it as the reincarnation of their dead ancestors. Many believed it to have supernatural wisdom and power. When the European settlers arrived, however, they had no such feelings about the bears—or, indeed, the Indians. Their main gripe against the bears was that they preyed on their livestock, although given their omnivorous diet, it is unlikely that the bears would have caused significant losses. The areas of North America that have seen the most intensive cattle farming and ranching are the regions from which the brown bear has been virtually eliminated.

A SHAMEFUL TRADE

Today, although the brown bear has full protection in the United States, poaching continues because many parts of the bear are still valued in parts of the world, notably in Asia. In the mid-1980s, a grizzly hide and head had a value running into thousands of dollars, while foreclaws, prized for jewelry, fetched prices of $100 or more. The most valuable part of the bear, however, is the gallbladder, attributed with medicinal and aphrodisiac powers by people in Asia. In the early 1990s, bears' gallbladders commanded the same price per gram as heroin in some areas. In Canada and Russia, brown bears have been found killed and left intact—save for their gallbladders. ∎

Bear-watching on Alaska's McNeil River. This sanctuary is a great success, with supervision by wardens and strict limits on visitor numbers.

INTO THE FUTURE

In spite of protection, brown bears still face an insecure future in many places. Continuing habitat destruction is pushing ever-decreasing bear populations into smaller areas. Not only are they losing vital resources, but numbers of available bears for breeding may not be enough to continue to produce a genetically strong community.

The only way to overcome this is to manage their remaining habitat. This may involve linking habitats that contain different populations so that they have access to one another, or placing more bears in any given area.

Although the brown bear possesses nothing like the stronghold it once did in Europe, there is awareness of its plight, and, in many areas, steps have been taken to ensure that the situation does not worsen. At the end of the 1980s, it was

PREDICTION

THE TIME FOR ACTION

"We already know enough about grizzly biology to save these bears. No matter what else we learn, we're not going to have grizzlies very long unless we preserve large enough tracts of good woodland habitat."

John Craighead, Ph.D., bear expert

estimated that outside of Russia, the countries that had the greatest numbers of brown bears were Norway (about 200 bears), Sweden (some 600), the former Yugoslavia (300), and Romania (nearly 4,000). All of these countries manage their bears carefully; in some places farmers are reimbursed if bears kill livestock. Hunting is allowed in some places, but this is carefully controlled.

In many ways, the United States is far ahead of Europe in plans to protect its remaining bears. Extensive research is carried out on the grizzlies in such parks as Yellowstone, where many of them are fitted with collars with radio transmitters. This allows the bears to be tracked and their bodily functions monitored. The grizzly bears in Yellowstone Park fitted with radio collars are all given numbers, and the park authorities keep thorough records on them. Some experts feel, however, that enough is known about the bears in order to save them. What is important now, they say, is to secure sufficient habitat—for without this, the bears have no chance of survival. ■

BEARS IN SPACE

In the mid-1970s, a greater understanding of the grizzly bear's preferred habitat in the United States was gained by a pioneering study involving tracking the bears by satellite. This allowed greater access over more extensive terrain than the more conventional research done by radiotelemetry. Both radiotelemetry and the satellite study were pioneered by John and Frank Craighead in Yellowstone National Park. The Landsat satellite was used to track grizzly habitat across millions of acres of ground described as "barely accessible wilderness." The computer was able to identify the different types of land—from alpine meadows to dense pine forest or vegetated and bare rock—inhabited at various times by grizzlies within this area. In fact, it identified eight specific rock and vegetation complexes and showed, too, the relative use by the grizzly of these different locations. Within the area studied, a 13,225-sq mile (34,250-sq km) area of western Montana, it was found that grizzlies had a preference for foraging the vegetated rock at about 8,800 ft (2,680 m).

BEARS IN EUROPE

Austria, Italy, Greece, France, and Spain are said to have a few brown bears in remote areas. Although the bears are protected in these countries, land development always seems to take priority over the animals' habitat needs. In 1994, a European Parliament (EP) report highlighted the bears' plight and demanded action to save them. But while the EP spent more than £2 million in 1993 on conserving brown bears, it spent more on other schemes that would threaten the bears. European Members of Parliament have asked that the EP assess the environmental impact of the projects it funds before allowing them to proceed.

Illustration Rachael Lockwood/Wildlife Art Agency

INDEX

Published by Marshall Cavendish Corporation
99 White Plains Road
Tarrytown, New York 10591-9001

© Marshall Cavendish Corporation, 1997
© Marshall Cavendish Ltd, 1994

The material in this series was first published in the English language by Marshall Cavendish Limited, of 119 Wardour Street, London W1V 3TD, England.

All rights reserved. No part of this book may be reproduced or utilized in any form or by any means electronic or mechanical, including photocopying, recording, or by any information storage and retrieval system, without prior written permission from the publisher and the copyright holders.

Library of Congress Cataloging-in-Publication Data

Encyclopedia of mammals.
    p. cm.
    Includes index.
    ISBN 0-7614-0575-5 (set)   ISBN 0-7614-0577-1 (v. 2)

    Summary: Detailed articles cover the history, anatomy, feeding habits, social structure, reproduction, territory, and current status of ninety-five mammals around the world.
    1. Mammals—Encyclopedias, Juvenile. [l. Mammals—Encyclopedias.] I. Marshall Cavendish Corporation.
    QL706.2.E54 1996
    599'.003—dc20
                                                                        96-17736
                                                                        CIP
                                                                        AC

Printed in Malaysia
Bound in U.S.A.

WITHDRAWAL